What The Sam Hill

Toby Swanson

DEDICATION

Dedicated to the mighty, mighty Eagles.

Published by Main Menu Press Now
2910 Westown Pkwy. Suite 104, West Des Moines, Iowa 50266

ACKNOWLEDGEMENTS

A special thank you is in order first to my trusted friends who have read parts of the manuscript to this book and being the true friends that they are, encouraged me to continue with this project. Also, I would like to thank the three individuals who were kind enough to provide the cover photos. These include Dr. Stephen Swanson of Burlington, Iowa; Ottie Garrett of Hitching Post Enterprises, Inc. in Kalona; and Kathy Bowermaster of the Division of Tourism, Iowa Dept. of Economic Development. A special thank you is also offered to Scott Lindsey of Des Moines for his time and effort in designing the cover to this book as well as doing the layout of the interior.

A special thanks to my secretary, Shelly Weller, who typed and re-typed the manuscript, without complaint, to the point where she can recite from memory the entire book backwards. Finally, a salute to Sandy Davis who walked into my office and picked up the manuscript and returned with the final product. I appreciate her expertise and guidance through this part of the project which would never have been done without her. Thank you one and all.

1

MORNING MOURNING

Ben Sardinhurst preferred conducting funerals out of doors. Since Sam Hill is near the middle of Iowa, this is not always possible. But Carl Carlson had passed away some time during the night in late June and the day of his funeral was perfect for picnics, swimming, baseball games and outdoor funerals.

The ladies of the Dorcas Society would not be attending the funeral because they were busy in the basement of the Methodist church preparing the sandwiches and punch for the mourners who would attend the service. Other absentee mourners included most of the octogenarians from Edna's retirement home. Many of them were good friends of Carl, who has spent his last few happy months at Edna's, but even though they were a spry lot for their advancing years, these services made them painfully aware of their own mortality.

Ben anticipated a goodly sized crowd, regardless of those who would not attend, because Carl had been a life long resident of Sam Hill and had left behind many friends. Often, those who live long lives outlive many of their friends and their good deeds are long forgotten by the time of their demise. However, Carl had devoted a great portion of his life not only in serving his peers, but he spent many Saturdays befriending the children of Sam Hill by coaching various AAU and little league teams. About the only time Ben remembered him absent from the Saturday morning social life of the youngsters was when he was in the coma.

As soon as Ben heard the news that Carl had passed away, he checked the forecast and then formulated plan "A". The forecast was accurate so plan "B", which was using the church in case of rain, did not become a factor. Plan "A" consisted of moving all the picnic tables and park benches from the park in town and the green area around the courthouse to the flat area behind Edna's retirement home between the pond and the woods.

This was the perfect place for the ceremony for several reasons. First, it was easy for Ben's father, the mayor, William Sardinhurst, to arrange for the picnic tables and benches to be moved by the three members of the city road maintenance crew. Carl had been their supervisor before he retired when Angel died and not only did they feel obligated to accommodate the preacher, but it was easy to back the city maintenance truck directly to the area where the benches and tables were placed. Next, this would be very accessible for Carl's elderly friends and neighbors at Edna's and it would encourage more of them to attend than might ordinarily be expected. Finally, the radio and newspaper announcement of the funeral locale advised the youngsters of Sam Hill that Edna's pond would be open for public fishing after the funeral service. The pond was normally restricted to the residents at the retirement home and their immediate family, so many of the children of Sam Hill encouraged their grandparents to retire at Edna's so they would have that the privilege of fishing at the well stocked pond, but since this would be a public fishing day, the crowd would swell with youngsters and their parents who were not lucky enough to have elderly family members living at Edna's.

Ben arranged the seating so that the mourners would be facing a southwesterly direction as they viewed the casket and Ben. This was important because the Sam Hill cemetery, where Carl's remains would be laid to rest next to Angel, could been seen less than a mile away, nestled on top of the hill which also happened to be the highest point in the county. It was that very cemetery hill that generations of Sam Hill boys and girls ran each day during cross country season. Carl himself, who for years had run home for lunch every day, had thus been an encouragement to the local harriers to condition their bodies by running up and down the cemetery hill.

The cemetery itself was divided into two sections. The first three deaths in the community, over a century before, were all people of the Catholic persuasion. Sam McDonough, his young wife Reeby and their infant child Tobias were all killed when Sam's horse, Pockets, reared and their buckboard flipped over crushing them. Sam was a very young man who had just brought his family to Iowa from Dublin. It was a most pathetic situation. Sam knew very little about horses or buckboards or surviving in a community so small and so new that it was still yet unnamed. It was a time before immigration quotas and green cards and perhaps that was too bad for Sam and his family. Had they been required to meet immigration requirements, perhaps they would have stayed in Dublin and their bloodline would still survive. On the other hand, it was rather fortunate for their legacy that the tragedy occurred, because after Sam, Reeby and little Tobias were interred, the town fathers referred to the new cemetery as Sam's Hill and soon thereafter, in his honor, the town was dubbed Sam Hill.

When the first Protestant died, there was a quick and quiet understanding that the final resting place for the Protestants should be on the other side of the hill. Both groups knew that the Lord would not be returning to redeem and resurrect those of the conflicting interpretation of scripture, so it was made easier for the Lord to awaken the sleeping souls entrenched together on one side of the cemetery as opposed to having to hunt from tombstone to tombstone.

So it is that the road to the cemetery forks out in three directions. The large section on the right with the huge cross at the entrance is still the Catholic section. The section to the left is where the Protestant bodies are buried and the road in the middle of the cemetery leads to the maintenance shed with a few handfuls of graves along the way. The Catholics had originally bought up the middle ground also, thinking that through conversion and strong advocacy of large families their numbers would far exceed those of the misinformed. However, as their family members left Sam Hill or became ex-communicated for various reasons, such as the case of Vern Bishop, who became bankrupt, some of the lots were sold and resold. Ultimately the agnostics, atheists, naturalists, humanists, and the rest whose world view clashed with the Protestants and Catholics purchased and used those lots.

William Sardinhurst arrived early. He wanted to make sure the city maintenance crew had put the park benches and picnic tables where Ben wanted them. As he surveyed the grounds, the physical setting appeared to be in order. The pallbearers carried the casket from the buggy to the position that Ben had requested. William briefly wondered why they were called pallbearers. Obviously they had a load to bear but he wasn't sure if the remains in the casket were a pall. He made a note to have Ben's wife, Cynthia, look that up at the library if she did not already know.

William remembered that this funeral was announced to be casual dress. The pallbearers were all wearing black ties but none had on a suit coat. The barber, Sal, was the only pallbearer who was unmarried. The wives of the other bearers of pall had checked them out and made sure that they were wearing either white or light blue shirts, except for Slug Marshall, the chief of police, who was in uniform and would double his duty after carrying the casket back to the horse and buggy for transportation to the cemetery. At that time he would jump in the police car and drive ahead of the procession as if John McNaughton, the mortician, and driver of the horse and buggy would need help in finding the nearby cemetery where he had personally delivered nearly one-fourth of its occupants.

William knew that no one would say anything to Sal, but he did look a little different with his bright flowered silk shirt that his mother had brought him from Hawaii. In case people would not know where the shirt came from, the word Hawaii was printed in large block letters several times on both the front and back of the shirt which hung out over Sal's pants. The shirt had brought good luck to Sal on his last two trips to Las Vegas. Each time he wore the shirt he came out ahead enough to offset losses on days the shirt was not worn. Sal didn't necessarily think there was anything lucky or unlucky about being asked to help carry the casket, but just in case any luck would rub off from this job probably it would not be good luck and Sal hoped that the shirt might keep any of that non-existent bad luck from becoming contagious.

Even though Sam Hill had more than its share of talented vocalists, it was very difficult at outdoor events to determine how well the voices would carry. Ben remembered a practical pointer in seminary that more than one good song had been lost to a swirling wind. Volume could be controlled much easier with taped music and quite frankly, Ben felt that professionally recorded music carried more impact than the sometimes off key renditions delivered by Sophie Peck, who was the best that Sam Hill could offer but who fortunately was also assigned to the sandwich detail at the Methodist church.

As the crowd began to assemble and Ben adjusted the volume of *His Eyes Are On The Sparrow,* he remembered another tidbit of practical wisdom from the same instructor. The mentor had counseled the fledgling pastors to the effect that other than Christmas and Easter services, there are only three opportunities to spread the gospel to a captive audience. Those were at the times of baptism, marriage and death. Ben had committed to memory this trilogy of life as the times when one is carried, married, and buried. Ben mused that the devil was striving to take away the preacher's opportunities. Modern society was finding marriage to be unpopular and as a result, the unwed couples were reluctant to present children born out of wedlock for baptism. The only remaining time to present the good news of the savior was at the funeral and of course at that time it was too late for the deceased. However, this event, like most, was not so much for the benefit of the principal, but must satisfy the audience, without which there would be no need for a presentation.

The final song before Ben's sermonette and eulogy was *The Old Rugged Cross.* By the time the final song started, the picnic tables and benches were filled and lawn chairs were spread throughout the vacant spots. Blankets were spread on the ground and teenagers and parents with young children made themselves comfortable.

As the words to the song started, Ben, neatly dressed in a white casual suit with a blue open collar shirt, placed one hand on the casket and turned away from the crowd and toward the cemetery. At that moment the words came forth from the speaker.

"ON A HILL FAR AWAY STOOD AN OLD RUGGED CROSS."

The crowd gasped as the large cross on the Catholic side of the cemetery, which was clearly visible under normal circumstances, changed hues from white to red to yellow to red again and then back to white. Ben did not need to turn around to feel the electrical charge exuded from the crowd as they watched in amazement. The strong believers knew that it was a sign from God, perhaps even the commencement of the rapture. The less strong in their faith were merely thankful to be witness to such an event while the skeptics knew that Slug Marshall's grandson was playing with the flashers in the police car which was parked near the horse and buggy out of their view, but in a perfect position where the flashing lights would reflect from the sun on to the cross at the cemetery.

The song continued and a few minutes later the crowd was again moved by the words.

"SO I'LL CHERISH THE OLD RUGGED CROSS TILL MY TROPHIES AT LAST I LAY DOWN."

The mayor looked up from his position next to Edna on one of the park benches near the middle of the gathering. His son was still standing with his back to the gathering as he watched the cross continue to change colors. Meanwhile, people were standing up and moving toward the casket as though there were an unannounced alter call. As William studied the situation more closely, it reminded him of the story of the Magi carrying gifts to the infant Christ child. However, these were not Magi and the gifts that were being brought were being tendered to Carl Carlson's casket. Sal reached into the breast pocket of his Hawaiian shirt and pulled out a pack of cigarettes. He walked to the casket and slid them into the inside breast pocket of Carl's suit coat. During the presentation of the body, William had noticed Carl was the only person who had violated the casual dress requirement, although Carl really didn't have any choice in the matter.

Next came the widow, Penelope Peaks, who carried what appeared to be an aluminum ring from a pop top beverage can. She approached the casket and slid the ring onto Carl's pinkie finger.

Finally, to William's embarrassment, Monica Monroe, a long legged bosomy nurse, who Edna hired fresh out of nursing school not long before Carl came out of his coma, appeared from one of the side doors of the retirement home where she had just been relieved by William's other daughter-in-law, Rachel. Monica was still in her full white uniform and was carrying a small two legged orange and white sidewalk barricade with an orange flasher attached. Imprinted on the side was the inscription

Property of Sam Hill Road Works

Monica set the barricade next to the casket and then gently put her arm around the widow Peaks. Sal took a few steps backward to be with the other bearers of pall and as the widow dabbed the wetness from her eyes with a kleenex, Monica placed an arm around her and gently guided her back to her folding chair. After making sure that Penelope was recomposed, Monica stood and stared at M.L. Ullestad, the city attorney, till their eyes locked. She raised her eyebrow as if directing a question to him. Ullestad, much older and wiser than the young nurse, simply smiled and shrugged his shoulders, thus answering, in kind, the non-verbalized question which had been transmitted to him. Monica smiled and then retreated to Edna's where she had some charts to finish.

Ben was still watching the cross in the distance and formulating for the final time the words that he was about to convey to the gathered flock.

2

DANCES WITH HORSES

Angel Emmanuel fell in love with Carl Carlson the day he lost his front teeth saving her life. She was only six years old at the time and Carl was a teenager, but her steadfast devotion paid off twelve years later when he returned from the battles of the South Pacific.

The seven best friends from the Sam Hill class of 1942 had volunteered for the remainder of the war. Carl and Alexander Grover both served in McArthur's arena. Joe Dermotts and Frank Peck had drawn desk jobs in San Diego while William Sardinhurst, M. L. Ullestad and Slug Marshall were under the command of George Patton. Grover was the only one of the young men to marry before entering the service and was also the only one to die during the war.

The same seven had all been born in Sam Hill and as youngsters spent many leisurely hours of childhood at the Carlson farm which was adjacent to the property that Grover's widow would eventually buy and where she would build her retirement home.

When the boys were about ten years old, Carl's father tied a worn out tire to a long rope and hung it to the large oak tree which partially shaded the Carlson farmhouse. Over the next few years many children played on the homemade swing, swinging back and forth, higher and higher, until the pit of their stomachs would tickle their tonsils.

Angel Emmanuel's parents were Amish. Actually, her father was Amish and her mother was a Quaker. Her father would not permit her mother to discuss the difference in their backgrounds so the family secret that Angel's mother was a Quaker was never discussed with Angel or the other children. Of course the neighbors whispered about this different family after the Emmanuels moved to Iowa from Pennsylvania but the other children easily accepted Angel and her brothers and sisters.

Angel's father was very rigid with his family. They traveled by the traditional horse and buggy. Angel and the other females in the family always wore black caps and their clothing never contained colors other than black and white.

It was a fine Sunday summer afternoon when Angel's father decided to pay a visit on his goodly neighbor, Mr. Carlson. He needed company for the journey and took Angel with him. His horse, High Pockets, was hitched to the buggy and within half an hour Mr. Emmanuel and Mr. Carlson were drinking coffee in the Carlson kitchen while Angel was playing with her doll in the buggy and High Pockets grazed on the unparched grass which was protected by the shade of the oak tree. The only sound other than the conversation Angel was having with her doll was the noise of Carl's hammer pounding nails into the garage that he was helping construct for the family's first car.

High Pockets was a direct descendant of the infamous Pockets, which had been spooked by a ground squirrel nearly a century earlier. The disposition of High Pockets was much more relaxed than that of his progenitor, but somewhere in the shuffle there had been a trade off and the intelligence of High Pockets was not very great, even by horse standards.

High Pockets became so absorbed in the grass that he never lifted his head and did not see the tire until after he bumped it with his neck. He then looked up and was surprised to see the round black rubber circle drape itself over his head. He then moved forward causing the tire to slip completely over his head and around his neck.

While Angel continued to play with her doll, High Pockets started getting nervous. He began walking in circles in a counter-clockwise fashion in a futile effort to remove the tire from his neck. As he walked in circles the rope tightened and put pressure on the poor creature's throat. As the pressure increased, High Pockets became less and less tolerant of the situation and increased his gait.

By the time Carl heard Angel's screams, the swing was so tight around High Pockets' neck that the poor horse was standing on its back legs to keep from chocking to death. Carl came racing around the house and first noticed that High Pockets' eyes were bulging out of his head and his chest was heaving, as the dumb animal tried to get oxygen. Green grass and white foam were being thrown into the air from the horse's mouth, looking like green and white frisbees flying through the air. The flailing front hooves of the horse were nearly head high to Carl, reminding him of his typing teacher at school, whose movements were so fast on the keyboard that it looked as if her hands were actually flying.

Luckily, even though the buggy's wheels were off the ground and the buggy was tilted backward, Angel had grabbed the reigns and was holding on for dear life to avoid falling out.

Carl immediately sensed that there was no time to find a knife or axe to cut the rope to the swing. Even if there had been time, such an action would have caused the horse to drop to the ground and little Angel would have been thrown under the horse and buggy in the free fall. So Carl took the only action which was available.

He charged the horse much as a boxer would charge his opponent when tired, trying to bear hug the opposition between blows. Carl grabbed the horse, dug his head against the animals huge chest and wrapped his arms around the horse, grabbing its mane. Thus positioned, he started pushing the horse into a clockwise motion, untangling the rope. The beast, unable to comprehend the logic of this movement, continued to follow its counterclockwise path. Angel watched in amazement as the young man and beast struggled.

The bizarre dance continued for many minutes. Eventually, the horse started to lose consciousness due to oxygen deprivation, and Carl was able to take control of the direction of his adversary. Finally, after six complete turns the rope was slackened enough so that the horse could stand on all four hooves without being choked.

It was only after the battle was over and the tire removed from the horse's head that Carl realized that High Pockets had caught him flush in the mouth at the beginning of the encounter and his two front teeth were lost in the remaining green grass in the shade of the oak tree.

3

LIVING IN PARADISE

Other than the skydiving debacle, Carl Carlson led what most people considered to be a rather drab life. His parents could not afford to have the missing teeth replaced and Angel enjoyed the physical evidence of his gallantry. Years later, even after Angel's departure, Carl's lack of ego allowed him to disregard the stares of strangers who sometimes would focus on his mouth. Otherwise, Carl would be described as neither attractive nor unattractive. He had average height and weight, a full head of straight auburn hair and brown eyes which, though bright and perceptive, did not attract attention.

After the incident with High Pockets, Angel would draw pictures for Carl every day. During the school year she would leave these in his locker and during the summertime they would be stuffed in the Carlson mailbox. They rode the same bus to school each day and even though the grade school youngsters were to sit toward the back, Angel always sat as close to Carl as the unwritten rules would allow.

She attended the high school baseball games and sat attentively behind the dugout watching Carl as he roamed in the outfield and concentrated at bat. Although William Sardinhurst and Slug Marshall were the best players, little Angel never took her eyes nor her heart off the grinning, toothless young man who had saved her life and tried to ignore the child's adorations.

Angel was nearly ten when Carl and his friends laid down their gloves and bats in response to their inner voices of patriotism and the various induction notices which they all received. For nearly the entire previous year the nation's focus on the war effort had not escaped even the children, so Angel did understand that the men of

Sam Hill were required to go away until the matter was resolved. To Angel's way of thinking, this was an inconvenience for Carl who would be gone for a while, like the time he went to Y Camp.

By now, her pictures had become letters and because mail was postage free to the servicemen, Angel was able to continue her daily devotions to Carl.

Although Carl and Alexander had not been extremely close when growing up, their friendship increased as they shared military experiences. Alexander good naturedly kidded Carl nearly daily about the letters received from the child Angel. Out of embarrassment, Carl threw away the painstakenly written letters, often without even more than scanning them. Edna wrote often to Alexander, but her letters somehow were less impassioned than those of the nubile maiden who was layered in the traditional clothing of her Amish-Quaker heritage.

Eventually, both men came to realize that the main link to the only world they had ever known was through the eyes and pen of a child, and there became a degree of gratefulness for the continuing and constant flow of both local information and concern for their safety as the child matured and came to a better understanding of their mission.

It was nearly two years from the date of their induction that Alexander Grover died within a few yards of Carl. When compared to death by a long, slow, lingering disease that attacks organ after organ, a bullet which immediately pulverizes and destroys the same organs seems preferable. However, as Carl lay pinned down in his fox hole unable to reach out and hold Alexander, who was screaming and crying with anguish for what seemed an eternity, such comparisons of dying were not relevant. The only thing that mattered to Carl at that moment was that he could not give comfort to his friend at that one time in life when comfort was most needed.

After Alexander's death, Carl discontinued his practice of discarding Angel's letters. No matter how much room they took, no matter what essential had to be discarded, her letters became a priority to him.

After the war was over, most of the young men who had left their roots but a few years earlier to find adventure and destiny now felt the urgency to return to that which they had left. Carl's world had changed, but unlike the vast majority of young men, he needed more time to reflect. He elected to receive his discharge at Pearl Harbor. He had never before written to Angel or acknowledged her attentions, but the letters mysteriously continued to find him.

He had written his parents and told them that he was staying indefinitely in Honolulu, living with other discharged soldiers in tents in Kapialani Park near Waikiki. About once every two weeks he would check into the Muana Hotel for a night to enjoy the amenities of a bath and bed with walls to insure solitude. No one in Sam Hill knew where he had these encounters with civilization but whenever he did indulge in the luxury of the hotel, there would be a packet of letters addressed to him in care of the Muana. Angels' letters were becoming more like a diary as she transformed through pubescence, holding back none of her unashamed love for him as only the innocent can do.

When Carl's discharge money ran out, he only occasioned the Muana to pick up his mail from Angel. He moved his tent to the top of Diamond Head and foraged the remaining natural vegetation for fruits and vegetables to survive. The natives showed him the reservoirs and falls where he found wai to drink. The cane fields furnished ko and often he would assist with the nets and receive, for his labor, 'ahi, 'ula, 'opae, and puhi.

Slowly but surely the island attracted haoles and tourists and Carl was forced to the windward side of the island. But the towns grew and Carl felt forced to move to the north shore where only the surfers and native Hawaiians relished the rugged forces of nature.

There were no seasons and no reasons for Carl to keep track of time. Eventually he traversed the Ko`olau mountains, heading south, and found himself back at the Muana. Almost six hundred letters were waiting for him. He had no idea he had been gone so long. Angel was now a senior in high school and her last letter contained her graduation picture. Even though her bonnet covered her hair and was pulled down over her ears, Carl could see that the child was transformed into a beautiful young woman. Although she had never, not even once requested that he return to her or Sam Hill, her messages always included prayers for his well being and safety no matter where he would be.

Carl then gave away his tent and sleeping bag which were his only possessions other than the letters from Angel. He then booked on as a cook on a tourist ship to pay for his passage back to the United States and within two weeks he was in Sam Hill.

4

MAIDEN HEAVEN

Sam Hill had not changed much over the years that Carl had been gone. There were a few new markers in the cemetery, while on the other end of the life-cycle the post war boom had been gracious to Sam Campbell, the local entrepreneur who had the foresight to go into the baby carriage business. Some years later, his son, Soupy, would convert the family retail outlet into a restaurant.

Carl had no family business to take over, so he took the first job which was available, working on the street crew in Sam Hill, a job which he would keep until retirement. He landed the job the third day that he was back from Hawaii and that was the same day that he first noticed the young woman in the traditional Amish garb watching him. She was standing across the street from his parents' home the first time he saw her. He next saw her standing on the corner steps of the courthouse as he leveled the concrete which replaced the red brick surface which had been on the towns main thoroughfare for as long as he could remember. She was still near the courthouse when he walked out of the first movie that he had seen in over five years.

On the third day he walked over to her. He stared at the three dimensional likeness of the picture she had sent him. Her face was more lovely than any picture could portray and her blue eyes melted as he ventured to glance at them. He knew everything that was in her heart and soul which she had opened and bared to him every day since she was six years old. She knew nothing about him, but she knew everything of him. She had slowly crept into his innermost being and he had no way of knowing whether she was aware of what she had done.

They had nothing in common. They had lived in the same town but had grown up in different periods of history. He had been exposed to the world and its pain had nearly broken him. She knew so very little of life. A school bus was the only engine driven machine in which she had ever ridden. Her family taught her to live without the luxuries of electricity and her work experience was limited to feeding High Pockets, still the family's mode of transportation. She had rarely been outside of Sam Hill while he had seen too much of the world. He knew nothing of her life but knew everything of her being. Carl could find no adequate way to express himself. The first words that he ever said to Angel were, "You are not in my debt because of what happened at my swing. You have paid me back many times over. You are free to go about your life, but if there is anything I can do for you please let me know."

Then, for the first time, Carl heard Angel's voice as she replied, "We must have my father's approval before you can marry me." With that, she turned and walked away, glancing back only three times at him before she disappeared around the corner, leaving him with a pounding in his heart.

Shortly after the marriage, Carl and Angel rented the unrefurbished house at 310 Baker Street, across the street from William and Eleanor Sardinhurst, who had been married about two years and in keeping with the baby boom spirit, had just had their first child, Barry. Carl wanted theirs to be a traditional marriage and was quite content to keep Angel from learning a trade. They saved on utility bills because the rewiring job which needed to be done before electricity could be restored was cancelled and eventually Carl became accustomed to the lifestyle without power that Angel had always known. Angel's parents had given the couple Son of High Pockets as a wedding present and the young couple fared very well using the horse and buggy for weekend rides and trips to the grocery store.

Although both Carl and Angel were soul mates and offered nothing but unconditional love to each other, something was amiss. The union and unity of the spirit was lacking in the flesh. They were deeply in love but both had a sense that the totality of their relationship was somehow incomplete.

There were two war widows in Sam Hill. Edna Grover had recovered from Alexander's demise and was busying herself with aspirations to develop a retirement home. The other widow was Penelope Peaks, a woman whose birth was some time between those of Carl and Angel. Penelope tried to busy herself in the library, a job she would maintain until many years later when Ben Sardinhurst's wife, Cynthia, would take the job. Penelope also lived on Baker Street, adjacent to the Carlsons. She had moved to Sam Hill from Des Moines after receiving news of the death of her husband and even though the new environment and job helped distract her from her hurt, she would reflect on her late husband whenever she saw Carl and his Amish-Quaker wife, survivors of those terrible war years.

On the weekends, when Carl was reliving and sharing the joys of the art of baseball with the little league team he had volunteered to coach, Penelope became friends with Angel and the friendship soon developed into a bond of trust between the two young women.

One day Angel, in her normal candor, asked Penelope if she had felt satisfied in all aspects of her marriage. Penelope had seen what a warm and tender relationship existed between Carl and Angel and knew that there could only be one thing that was separating them from the best of marriages. That night Penelope made a special trip to the library and brought back three books from the top shelf of the back room where children were not allowed to peruse.

The following week Angel studied the books, one of which was illustrated. Penelope answered questions that Angel had and explained things to Angel that Angel was too embarrassed to ask.

The following week Carl had a long lunch hour scheduled so he told Angel not to make him a sack lunch but he would stop home to eat with her. Much to his surprise and shock, when he entered the kitchen, Angel was standing by the wood burning stove wearing her Amish-Quaker bonnet and an apron. And that was all. Carl sat down and stared at the plate with its meager sandwich and lettuce salad. He was afraid to lift his eyes. When Angel delivered a glass of water to him and then walked away from him toward the kitchen sink, he could see that her back side was covered only by the apron string. Carl could no longer think of the food so he mumbled something, got up and left.

That night Carl was home very early. And the next day he was late to work for the first time since he had gone to work for the street department. Within a week Carl took up jogging and started running back and forth from work to home over the noon hour for lunch. Penelope saw Angel less and less because Carl, other than the required time at work, was always at home with Angel. Carl nearly quit teaching little league but Angel did convince him that they must continue to share part of their lives with other people. It was during these practices over the next few years that Angel would have her infrequent opportunities to meet and share with her other soul mate in life, Penelope, the miraculous and wonderful stories of her perfect marriage with Carl.

5

JUMPING FOR JOY

Carl and Angel were so happy that they hardly noticed as the days slipped into months and the months passed into years. Sometimes on Sundays, after Angel and Penelope had enjoyed their Saturday morning conversations, Penelope's car could be seen leaving for Des Moines shortly after church. Later that afternoon, she would return, with a brown paper bag. The contents of the bag would later be given to Angel and shortly thereafter Carl could be counted upon to run home a little faster over the lunch hour.

On their fourteenth wedding anniversary, Carl and Angel hitched up the buggy to Deep Pockets, another direct descendant of the infamous Pockets, and went for a picnic. They stopped near the airport and watched in amazement as little Barry Sardinhurst parachuted out of Slug Marshall's new single engine Cessna. Actually, the plane was on loan for a trial basis to the town of Sam Hill as Slug, who had recently been elected sheriff, had convinced the city council that certain streetwise criminals from Des Moines were harvesting marijuana from the cornfields near the Johnson farm and a plane would be necessary to maintain surveillance of the area. All of the council members knew that the city did not have the funds to purchase a police airplane, but the new mayor, William Sardinhurst, suggested a thirty day trial basis for the plane with the understanding that his oldest son, Barry, who had an adventuresome spirit, could use the plane to try this novel new sport.

Barry had been on Carl's little league baseball team for the past couple years. Barry was probably a better athlete than his father had been and he, and Rex Smalley, a goodly sized catcher who had bloodlines stretching into the major leagues, made for the best battery in the state. Barry's younger brother, Ben, was also a natural gifted athlete but his youth relegated him to the outfield on Carl's team. Sal Salmons was also on the team, but he preferred playing cards in the dugout to learning the fine art of the game. Herm Sherman played a decent third base, but was often day dreaming about his favorite sport - fishing.

The boys had learned much about the game from Carl, who had been their coach for the preceding four years. Every Saturday morning from early spring until school started, Carl would be the surrogate father to the members of his team. On those days when the weather was too wet for playing, the team would meet with Carl in the game room of the YMCA and when the boys tired of discussions of strategies and baseball situations, Carl would tell them stories of the South Pacific.

There were two problems which arose when Carl would talk to the boys about his life experiences. First, Carl's communication skills were less than perfect except when he was with Angel who could understand everything about him without the need of verbal expression. Secondly, some of the children, especially Rex Smalley, were not blessed with auditory communicative excellence. Thus, when Carl interspersed his stories of the dangers of the war years with his self-exiled rehabilitation in Hawaii, much of it came out garbled in Rex's mind. Thus, when Rex opted for self-destruction many years later, he chose Hawaii because he mistakenly thought that the land of paradise was where Carl had confronted many dangers.

Angel and Carl marveled at Slug as he would rev up the engine until it sounded as if it would burst. The plane would then burn rubber down the runway and somehow gracefully elevate itself into the rich blue summer sky. Soon thereafter a small image would jump spread eagle from the plane and as it accelerated downward, strings would appear and the parachute would snap the hurling body into an upright position and Barry would slowly and gracefully descend. Without speaking, Carl's eyes and gaping mouth with its missing teeth told Angel everything. Without hesitation, she ran to Barry and asked if Carl could jump from the plane. The rest of the afternoon marking the fourteenth anniversary of Carl and Angel's wedding was spent with the young baseball player and his coach alternating parachute jumps as Slug happily piloted the two.

Even though it would have been a surprise if the boys had not won a state little league tournament, the parents wanted to give a special gift to the boys and Carl for all their efforts. A trip to Chicago was planned so that the team, parents and coach could see a major league game in Wrigley Field. It would be a special treat for Carl, since many of the parents were friends of his since pre-school years and he had been privileged to coach their children when he and Angel had none of their own. Some of Carl's friends thought that the reason Carl and Angel had no children was because of her religious background, which when translated meant that they didn't have children because they probably didn't do what was necessary to conceive.

The bus trip to Chicago took a full day and that night while most of the boys and their parents were fast asleep in their hotel rooms, Carl and Angel, among other things, came up with an idea that would add extra fun to the next day's activities at the ball park.

The next day everyone arrived early to watch batting practice. The group from Sam Hill had tickets on the left field line just beyond the Cubs bullpen. Between the joys of running back and forth for the hot dogs and soda, and anticipation of batting practice balls being slammed into the area, no one noticed that Carl was not with the group. Even as the game time drew close and the stringy haired girl who could have barely been out of college approached the microphone to sing the national anthem, Carl's absence was still unnoticed.

The singer, who wore a dress which looked like a flag draped around her, was accompanied by two steel guitar players. Even though a new involvement in Southeast Asia was transpiring, this was not a concern to most people in America at that time but apparently the young singer was making some political protest as she sang our great national song in a manner in which the Sam Hill people had never heard. To them, the nation's song had always been played and sung one way with the only variation being that nobody could really carry the tune properly. This young girl with heavy metal made the song seem to come from another planet, with her screeching high notes and drawn out low sounds.

The Sam Hill contingent was still buzzing about the strangeness of the national anthem when the airplane first started circling the stadium. A long banner trailed the small plane and as it circled directly over the field, everyone could see that the banner congratulated the Sam Hill little league team for winning it's state championship.

The players had just left the Cubs dugout to take the field when the door of the airplane opened and a tiny figure jumped spread eagle from the plane. The jumper did not take into consideration the strong winds that were blowing in off Lake Michigan that day and by the time Carl's parachute opened, he was heading off the course which was designed to land him in center field and in fact he was drifting out of the stadium toward Waveland Avenue.

The players stopped dead in their tracks and their eyes, along with the eyes of the coaches, managers, ushers, vendors, and eighteen thousand fans, not to mention the two bat boys, singer and guitar players, watched as Carl beat the air with his arms, flailing like a fish out of water, in an effort to prevent himself from crashing into the fire station across the street.

The left field foul pole in Wrigley Field is about forty feet into the air. Carl's parachute caught the tip of the foul pole and twisted him around, pulling him back toward the playing field. Only Carl and Angel, at that moment, thought about the incident with High Pockets. But this time, instead of Carl grabbing the horse and twisting him loose from the swing, it was Carl's turn to twist and shout as he hung about thirty-five feet above the playing field. As Carl turned and twisted, the parachute began to slowly tear. Carl could feel himself dropping an inch at a time. He looked down and saw where he would ultimately fall on the ivy covered brick fence and then tumble to the ground, either dead or broken into many pieces. There was a hush over the entire crowd as it appeared nothing could be done to save Carl.

As Carl was twisting toward the center field area, he could not see what was happening behind him but he heard a large gasp. As he rotated back to his right he could see a teenager who was wearing a Cubs jersey with number fourteen on it. The boy was one of only two people in the entire stadium to realize that there was a possible, though slim, chance of saving Carl.

The pole from which Carl was hanging was too slick to shimmy or climb, but Barry Sardinhurst saw the long guide wire that stretched from the protective net behind home plate all the way to the left field corner. He ran from his seat to the top of the brick wall that abutted the foul line along left field and using all of his athletic ability, leaped as high as he could and grabbed hold of the guide wire. He then pulled his body up and hooked his ankles around the wire and, monkey like, pulled himself upward, hand over hand. When he got as high as Carl's body, he was still about four feet away. He then held very tight with one hand while he reached in his pocket and took out his Swiss army knife which his father had given him for his latest birthday. He had meant to give it to Slug Marshall for taking him on the airplane rides, but he had not yet done so and he made a mental note to do that before much longer. He opened the knife and reached out as far as he could toward Carl but he was still about a foot short of being able to cut the lines of the parachute which held Carl in his perilous position.

Barry then watched as a young man with a crew cut and University of Alabama letter jacket jumped over the right field wall and started across the field. The singer cried out, with a drawl, "Run fast, Forrest! Run fast!" As quick as lightning the young man arrived at the wire which Barry had shimmied. Barry watched the young man climb on Rex Smalley's back and grab the wire and then start shaking it back and forth so that Barry could swing closer to Carl. Slowly but surely the taut wire began to sway back and forth. Barry's sharp knife jabbed at the nylon but it was very strong and resistant to his attempts to cut it. Minute after minute went by as Barry continued to swing back and forth swiping at the nylon.

All eyes were fixed on the action in deep left field. The umpires had even walked to the base of the foul pole so that they could determine if Carl would be in or out of the playing field when his body would fall to the earth.

Finally, Barry's knife completely cut one of the two remaining cords which held Carl in defiance of gravity. Barry knew that the easy part of the mission had been accomplished and that the next maneuver would either allow Carl to escape or would result in his demise. Barry looked down at the pride of the Crimson Tide and nodded. The Alabaman gave one big pull to the right and as Barry was swaying away from Carl he yelled, "Get ready to grab me."

As Barry reached the top of the arc and started coming downward in a direction toward Carl he took the knife and flung it just over Carl's head. The knife split the remaining cord and as the parachute started to release Carl from its tenuous grasp, Carl reached his arm to the right and caught Barry's wrist as Barry came toward him. Carl's weight jerked Barry loose and both bodies started toward the ground. Barry's strong legs were tightly wrapped around the wire, however, and it gave ever so slightly as Barry hung on upside down with Carl hanging vertically onto one wrist. Barry took his other arm and grabbed Carl's forearm and then felt his skin being rubbed off as their combined weight pulled them downward along the guide wire.

As they slowly came down the wire, a huge sigh of relief swept through the crowd. The young man from Alabama jumped down from Rex Smalley's large shoulders and dashed back toward his bleacher seat in right field, to re-join other army inductees in that area. As he sped across the field, a ping pong paddle fell out of the rear pocket of his trousers and the soprano's southern accented voice could be heard on the field microphone saying, "Run fast, Forrest, run fast!"

6

A REAL ANGEL

The ensuing years went by so quickly that Carl and Angel hardly noticed. Carl's friends were becoming in-laws and grandparents. His baseball teams were through school and had gone their own ways. Some, like Herm Sherman, went to a new war on an old battleground, and returned no better than, and probably worse, than Carl and his counterparts. Barry Sardinhurst, who married early, for some reason that Carl never fully understood, left his wife, Rachel, shortly after the death of their young son. Rex Smalley had given up an opportunity to play professional ball, and after his marriage to Roseanne, hired on as a chicken plucker at the plant on the edge of town.

Joe Dermott's niece, Phyllis Noble, the batgirl, temporarily took over the newspaper after Joe retired, but she was fraught with ambition and Carl remembered that she went abroad to study and write. As a matter of fact, she had collaborated on a book with Eric Erickson, who was best friends with Barry Sardinhurst and who spent most of his little league career as a substitute player and official score keeper. Slug Marshall had become a grandfather and in keeping with family tradition, the third generation Marshall was named Slug III. Bill Sardinhurst's younger son, Ben, had gone away for some time to the seminary but he came back and ministered to those Sam Hillians who chose to stay with their roots. Ben and his wife, Cindy, who was taking over Penelope's position at the library, had seven children and since their prosperity was more spiritual than material, they lived with Ben's parents at 321 Baker Street. Ben and Cindy's children were so well behaved that their uneventful lives did not even receive mention in most of the chronicles of Sam Hill.

The worst day of Carl's life was the same day that Slug Marshall mentioned over coffee with the city crew that Herm Sherman had gone off the deep end and probably killed somebody. As usual, Carl was racing home for his lunch hour and among other things wanted to share this bit of local gossip with Angel. However, when he entered the kitchen she was not waiting for him in one of her usual outfits which normally consisted of her bonnet and lacy negligee. Instead, she was in her black and white full length cotton dress and tear stains lined her cheeks.

She had been to see Dr. Goodman and he confirmed her worst suspicions. She had an advanced case of cancer of the uterus. Carl had often felt regret at being unable to console Alexander in his last moments. He was determined it would be different with Angel. As her illness progressed, drawing her energies and strength and feeding on her insides with a voracious appetite, Carl could feel himself dying with her. They had shared the best of times and now they agonized together through the worst of times. Carl caressed her, consoled her, cared for her and did everything humanly possible to make her comfortable during the next few weeks. Carl shivered in pain as the hours, minutes and seconds slowly dragged by. Each day of her illness lasted longer than each of the years that they had joyfully spent together. Finally, on a Thursday, he held her wasted body for the last time.

The following Monday, Angel's remains were transported to the cemetery in the family buggy. As her coffin was being lowered into the plot which Carl had purchased, an anxiety attack came upon Carl and he started gasping for air. Sal Salmons, who was one of the pall-bearers, did the only thing he could think of at the time. He took a cigarette from his pocket and as Carl was gasping for air, he placed it in the opening where Carl had no teeth. Sal lit the cigarette and Carl started drawing the smoke into his lungs. It stopped the anxiety attack, but it started a habit which put him in a coma on the second anniversary of the revival and marathon week-end.....

7

A PHONE CALL FROM CINDY

Eric Erickson had just finished work on the beach. He could feel the grit and sand in his hair and was looking forward to a shower as he turned the key to enter his condo just off Kuhio Avenue. The phone was ringing as he opened the door. After slipping off his sandals and tossing off his tee shirt, the phone was on its fourth or fifth ring when he picked it up.

It was Cynthia Sardinhurst. She had been his high school sweetheart but eventually married his best friend's little brother. They were still living in Sam Hill although Eric hadn't seen Cindy since he was back home a couple of years ago. After a few pleasantries she got to the point.

"Eric, are you aware that a book has been published about Francesca Johnson's affair?"

"I'm not sure, what about it?" he hedged.

He heard Cindy take a deep breath and then she continued, "The book is called *The Bridges of Madison County*. It's all about Francesca and Robert Kincaid. Apparently after her death, her daughter, Carolyn Johnson-Rogers, came across some letters and documents and told the story to some writer who is making a best seller of it. They even tracked down Kincaid and tried to find out as much as they could about his life."

Eric's stomach churned and his knees started to buckle. He sat on the floor and said, "Cindy, I did hear about the book but I had no idea it was that extensive. Was there any mention of why Kincaid was in Iowa?"

"It appears that they think he was here from *National Geographic* to shoot photos of the bridges around Winterset."

"Cindy, be completely honest with me. How many people know about our meetings with Kincaid?"

She paused for a moment. He didn't know if she was honestly trying to think if she had told anyone else or if she was preparing to lie. Finally, she said, "You and I and Barry were the only ones to meet with him. Even after I married Ben, I never told him nor anyone else about this. I don't know how much your mother knew or who she told, if anyone, and that would be my biggest concern."

There must have been two minutes of silence as each pondered the consequences of where this could lead. Finally, Cindy said, "Eric, I'm sure you've heard that we're having a marathon and revival in a few weeks. Sal Salmons arranged to have it combined with a meeting of hundreds of motorcycle riders who are scheduled to come through on their way to their annual rally at Sturgis, South Dakota. Eleanor is hinting that Barry may decide to drop into town. I really feel you should be back. Even if he doesn't show up, it is still important to find out if there are any rumors or knowledge about the Kincaid matter. If Barry does come back, you and I both know that things could get complicated."

Eric closed his eyes and rolled over. "Cindy, I'll plan on being back."

He picked up the orange tee shirt off the floor and looked at the white lettering which said BUT THIS IS MY DAY JOB. As he threw the shirt into the dirty laundry pile he wondered if it might be better to avoid going back to the mainland. What he did not know was that the conversation with Cindy had been recorded and that three men in dark suits and sunglasses were already receiving orders dispatching them from Washington, D.C. to a little town in Iowa called Sam Hill.

8

THE DORCAS SOCIETY

Even for Iowa, it was a hot August. The First United Methodist Church in Sam Hill had no air-conditioning and the deodorant was beginning to fail the women of the local Dorcas Society, who had gathered in the basement for prayers, projects and perhaps a pittance of gossip. The eight steadfast souls who arose at dawn to beat the heat had spent nearly two hours in the spacious room, but it was becoming apparent that the rising temperature would necessitate an earlier than hoped for ending to the meeting.

Marie Witherspoon pushed her bottom lip outward and blew the falling strands of white hair back to the general direction of the top of her head. Her cool expiration made her realize there were tiny beads of perspiration on her forehead. Marie was for now the most average of the group. She just turned sixty-eight (average), had her white hair mostly pulled back (not quite average-most of the women of the group were into a light purple tint-the other noticeable exception being Eleanor Sardinhurst, the mayor's wife, who never lost one strand of her coal black hair to gray, white or purple) and Marie suffered from the average number of maladies. She had Bright's disease, floating kidneys, and arthritis attacked her joints. Today her feet ached so she loosened the white nursing shoes she borrowed from her daughter Rachel, who shared the same shoe size.

Slowly she shifted her slightly rotund (average for this group) body so that her ankles touched the cool concrete floor. She viewed the small circle of large women and noticed with minor annoyance that every one of them was too large for the chairs. She took a close look at the chairs and realized to her chagrin that the ornery janitor had not mistakenly put out the children's chairs.

30

Marie closed her eyes. Her mind wandered. She could feel the heat of the desert and the sound of the war-whooping Indians as they approached the wagon train. Her late husband's voice was screaming at the women to get the circle smaller so the Indians couldn't get to the children. But it was hopeless. The derrieres of the women hung out too far and the wagons couldn't get any closer. Her ankle turned slightly and the cool touch of the floor brought her back to the meeting.

Edna Grover was to Marie's right. Edna was the only other widow of the group. Her husband, Pvt. Alexander Grover, was killed while storming a beach in the South Pacific for General MacArthur. Edna received a new flag, a nice medal and plaque from the military. Alexander had been a life insurance salesman before his war and had the foresight to recognize that while generals may vow to return, the same prerogative is not always available to privates. Thus, his insurance portfolio was loaded to the brim. Edna cashed in the insurance and built the Home for the Elderly four blocks from the courthouse just on the outskirts of town. She had owned and operated the establishment for well over thirty years now and was proud of the fact that she had never received a negative comment from the state Department of Health, nor had she ever spent more than a weekend away from her friends and patients.

Edna looked at her watch and saw that Minnie's face was covered by the beads of water caused by the humidity. One of the patient's grandchildren had brought her the watch from Disneyland or Disney world and Edna hoped it would dry out. She also hoped the air-conditioning would hold out today at the Home. She began to feel uncomfortable and wished that someone would suggest saying the closing prayer. After all, the weekend activities were less than three days away and everyone had much to do.

The body language of the remaining women made it quite clear that the Dorcas Society had spent itself this day. The discussions had been brief and long silences had prevailed. Eleanor Sardinhurst usually was expected to take charge when things dissipated, and this was no exception.

"Ladies, due to the heat, the number of other commitments that each of us has for the next few days, and because we have seemed to accomplish all that we can today, I would suggest that we submit our prayer requests for the week and then I will close our meeting with prayer," Eleanor stated quite authoritatively as expected.

Eleanor took a pad and pencil from her purse. She pointed the pencil, like a microphone, at each of the other women. Edna, hoping to expedite the conclusion, shook her head. Marie was off in another trance, and the pencil did not even make a complete stop at her. The other five women felt it either important enough or duty-bound to suggest certain petitions. Eleanor jotted as they spoke.

Valerie Salmon suggested a prayer for the economic condition of the community. Her son, Sal, was the town's only certified barber and beautician. Although that in no way certified him to be an economist, he was well trusted and appointed by the town's marathon and revival festival committee to be guardian of the finances. When the original committee was first organized almost a year earlier, no one imagined the peril that Sam Hill, like other agriculturally dependent communities, would be in. As times became worse for most folks, the committee knew the town's only chance would be through visitors. Events were needed. Big events. To draw literally thousands of spending spectators and participants to town. As dreams became possible realities, the financing problems for Sal became obviously beyond his abilities. It was obvious to his mother, anyway. She was aware that Sal had enjoyed his occasional junkets to Nevada and she hoped the town funds were secure. To her, everyone else seemed too busy with their own work to worry about Sal and the finances so she requested this prayer to remind them that her irresponsible son needed help. Lillian Marshall asked that they remember the law-enforcement officers during what would be the next few frantic days. Her husband, Slug, was chief of police. Lillian knew that Eleanor's son, Barry, saved their son, Slug II, one time and Eleanor's husband, Bill, the mayor, helped Slug get the promotion to chief. The kindnesses to Slug were certainly never flaunted by the mayor or his family; that's just the way things work when small town neighbors spend their lives together. Elsie Campbell said, "Please pray for all our children." The other seven women thought that Elsie was reminding them of her son's success. Elsie's son, Soupy, took over his father's baby carriage business several years before and converted it to a corner cafe, which became the only international business in town. He created a recipe for tomato soup that was unparalleled. Soupy was considered the only rich person in town and assuredly it would greatly add to his personal wealth if the crowds would come. Judge Frank R. Peck's wife, Sophie, quietly pleaded, "May that horrible trial be continued until Frank retires. I don't think he can handle it what with his other health problems." She openly sobbed. Eleanor wrote on the pad, CALL AA FOR FRANK AGAIN. An asterisk was placed by the notation to remind her not to mention this aloud when praying. Sophie was being consoled by her dear friend, Esther Ullestad, wife of the county attorney. Their husbands shared the same profession for many years now and the women empathized powerfully. Esther nodded to Eleanor and softly said, "My request is the same as Sophie's."

Eleanor looked at the list. Disregarding the asterisk, the list read, "town finances, cops, kids, trial." She figured she could make a prayer from that list easily enough. She put the pad on her lap, folded her hands and upon that cue, the others bowed in silence. Eleanor began, "Dear Father in heaven, you already know our hearts and have heard our prayerful requests. Please help our little town this week during the festival. We ask your help with Sal and the finances, with Slug and the law enforcement problems that may arise with such a large gathering, with our officers of the court as they complete their duties, and watch over our children...." Eleanor glanced at Elsie, then at Marie. She considered for another moment, then continued, "and Lord, that includes all of our children, even your prodigals. Grant us the strength to forget and forgive any of these who may return from exile."

There would be no amen to this prayer. All the women, in unison, opened their mouths and with wide-eyes gaped at Eleanor. Then all eyes turned toward Marie, whose eyes rolled up and out of sight as she slid off her small chair onto the cool floor.

9

CORN COBS AND WATERMELONS

William and Eleanor Sardinhurst had two sons, Barry and Benjamin, who was always called Benny or Ben. From kindergarten roundup through Barry's disappearance and apparent abandonment of his wife, Barry and Eric were the best buddies. After puberty, the twosome became a foursome with Cindy Bell and Rachel Witherspoon always with or near the boys. One of the things that attracted Cindy and Rachel to Barry and Eric was the fact that they always seemed to be care free and happy-go-lucky. Rachel and Cindy were a year behind the boys in school, as it is supposed to be among couples that age.

Even though Benny was only a couple of years behind the girls, it always seemed strange that Cindy would eventually marry the younger man. Perhaps the strangest part of her falling in love with Benny was that he was so different from his older brother. He always seemed content to stay at home and had an overwhelming concern for the spiritual welfare of other people.

During his senior year in high school, Barry managed to both distinguish himself as a hero and incur the wrath of the community (or at least Marie Witherspoon) within a span of a very few months.

The first incident started at the corn cob pile near the railroad tracks about three blocks from the town square and about a block from the football field. The corn cobs were delivered by railroad cars from all over the state and were put in a huge pile to dry so that they could be used in the process of making nylon. It was probably the biggest pile of cobs in the state and to the Sam Hill folks way of thinking was larger than a small mountain. In fact it was over a block long and nearly seventy feet high and measured one hundred feet wide.

About two weeks after school started, on a mild Indian summer type day, the noon hour siren sounded at half past the hour indicating a fire, and the engine screamed down the street heading to the cob pile. Carl Carlson and the rest of the volunteer firemen from around town either ran or drove to the scene to find a volcanic effect with flames shooting up from the middle of the pile.

Three junior high boys were lying at the bottom of the pile of cobs. They were already covered with soot and were coughing and in obvious distress. As Carl pulled the boys away from the cob pile and toweled down their faces, they pointed upward toward the blazing inferno and screamed that one of their friends was trapped in the fire. It was obvious that no one could survive the heat which was building and spreading throughout the entire pile.

As the impact of the tragedy was setting in among the helpless crowd that was gathering, a figure appeared from the back side of the pile and approached the stunned group. It was a rather tall, gangly figure carrying a charcoal colored smaller body around his neck. As he rolled the youngster off his shoulders onto the grass in front of Carl, Barry looked up and through his soot covered face said, "He ain't heavy, but he's a bother."[1]

Barry never talked about the incident, but the younger boys admitted that they had been smoking cigarettes on top of the cob pile when the fire started. Three of the boys managed to roll down the pile as the fire was spreading, but the fourth, Jud (Slug II) Marshall, sunk to his waist in the cobs and appeared to be doomed. Barry had seen the flames and apparently arrived a few minutes before the fire truck and volunteers. He scampered straight up the side of the cob pile and pulled out the boy who was already nearly unconscious from the flames' toxins. It was quite an incredible fire. The department volunteers knew that this was more than they could handle and after caring for the boys there was nothing that could be done except to watch the fire burn itself out over the next two weeks. The skies at night were lit like the aurora borealis. The homecoming rally was moved to the foot of the raging fire and many families assembled with folding chairs over the next weekends so that they could gaze at the spectacular fire. The chief of the fire department had urged Barry's father, the mayor, to take action against the boys for starting the fire. However, young Marshall's dad, Slug, was new on the police force and the mayor felt the rookie's son had been punished enough by nearly being toasted. So instead of handing out a reprimand, the mayor fashioned a corn cob pipe from one of the few remaining cobs and presented it to Slug to hand down through the generations as a memento from the time that Slug II had nearly died.

The cob pile was not the only thing that was generating heat. Barry was a celebrity of some sort and Rachel felt that it was time for a proper reward for him. She decided the gift would be offered by the hot cobs. Later, in one of those man to man, buddy to buddy talks, Barry told Eric that a few nights earlier he and Rachel made love for the first time and they were so close to the burning cobs that the heat from the fire scorched their hot flesh. Shortly thereafter, the couple agreed that they should do it again. That time they went to Cy Simms' watermelon patch. The melon season was over and everyone was tired of stealing and eating Cy's watermelons this late in the year so there was no one to interrupt their pleasures. The popular story which had been around forever was that Cy had a shotgun with salt pellets and was not afraid to use it on those invaders of his melon patch. The driving forces of passion surpassed the fear of the salt pellets, however, as the young lovers stayed in the patch untill well past midnight.

Although myths such as Cy's pellet gun are stuff with which small towns are made, it is no myth that Cy's wife bore her first and only child many years later at an age when most women are sharing stories of their grandchildren. The youngster grew tall and thin and was nicknamed Slim. A few years ago Slim established several local track records which will probably stand in this area of the state for some time. No one knew why Slim Simms had such a gift for running because Cy was a rather large rotund man and Slim's mother was so old by the time he reached high school that no one could remember her physical make-up as a young woman. The truth of the matter is that when Slim was going through adolescence, his father told the missus to explain the facts of life to Slim. Since she was advancing in years and had never had this conversation with a child before, and mostly because of that natural reluctance between parents and children to acknowledge the sexuality of each other, Mrs. Simms awkwardly and quickly told him that she had eaten one of the watermelons from her husband's famous patch and one of the seeds slipped through her stomach into her womb where it attached and became the baby that was ultimately born and now known as Slim. Then the subject was closed and she walked quickly away never to mention it again. However, poor Slim, thinking that he was half watermelon, became determined to run as fast as he could so that he would never develop the full-figureness of his father, the watermelon seed sower. Anyway, Rachel must have swallowed a watermelon seed either at the base of the cob pile or in the melon patch because a few weeks later she gave the news to Barry that they probably should discuss matrimony.

There was a full school assembly for all the school people, business folks and parents one crisp morning about the middle of November. The Governor came to town from Des Moines and several newspaper people were gathered to see the ceremony where Barry would be presented with a medal for the life saving episode. The only problem was that on the day of the ceremony, Barry was hitchhiking to Mexico where he needed to take a few days to sort out how he should handle the news from Rachel.

1. This quote was recorded in the September 15, 1963 edition of the Sam Hill Clarion. The story was covered and written by cub reporter Joe Dermotts.

10

WEDNESDAY

The library was empty, which gave Cindy time to look out the windows which flanked the main door, giving her a perfect view of the south side of the courthouse. As in all county seats, the courthouse was the centerpiece of the downtown area. The library was located on the southwesterly corner of the town square and across the street Cindy could see people scurrying in the clerk's office on the ground floor, and she could also peruse the goings on in the offices of the sheriff and county attorney on the second floor and the chambers of judge Peck on the third floor. The courthouse, like most buildings in Sam Hill, had been restored rather than restructured after the passage of a controversial bond issue some years earlier. Fortunately, the restoration was completed and the bond retired before the local land owners became unable to pay their real estate taxes resulting in both the county and town treasury becoming unable to meet budgets. Cindy could see the profile of judge Peck as he sat in his chair apparently lecturing M.L. Ullestad. She figured the judge was probably lecturing Ullestad for not accepting a plea bargain offer from Dr. Kellem, who was about to go on trial for committing abortions past the acknowledged time of viability.

The state legislature had structured a statute the previous year which was specifically aimed at Kellem who advertised openly on television that he would terminate pregnancies well into the last trimester. Although his clinic was on the outskirts of town beyond Edna's retirement home, most of Kellem's patients came from Des Moines which is less than an hour's drive. Most of the young and pregnant girls of the surrounding small towns such as Winterset and

Indianola were of such an upbringing as to carry their children to term and face the options of raising the young ones or letting them be adopted out, while many of the city girls shared a differing value system.

Kellem had defied the new state law and was now charged with one violation, although everyone agreed that probably hundreds of other violations could also be charged if the state so desired. Kellem's attorney had requested a fine in exchange for a no contest plea but Ullestad felt the pressure of the legislature and the religious right and he was determined to take this test case all the way through trial. He decided to let the jury first deal with it and if necessary, the appellate courts could next wrestle with this problem.

Judge Peck was within a few weeks of retirement and did not want the responsibility of taking this trial because of the publicity that was involved and the fact that he hated to be reversed by higher courts which was becoming all too often a fact of life for him. The judge had pleaded and urged Ullestad to cut the deal with Kellem's lawyer but it was becoming painfully obvious that a trial would go on and Peck now knew that he would need to go through this last trial even though he would much rather be out on Edna's pond. His greatest pleasure in life was there in his row boat with his drinking buddy, Joe Dermotts, his faithful bottle of gin and his favorite fishing pole.

Cindy turned her head from the courthouse and looked up the street to the Soup Kitchen which was on the northwest corner of the square. A couple of the high school boys were out front washing the windows and preparing to post the menu of the day in the window. Although the restaurant was always busy, the next two days would be especially busy with the beginning of the trial and all of the people coming in for the weekend celebration.

Inside the restaurant Soupy was busily stirring up his famous soup. The ingredients were so secret that no one else was allowed in the kitchen while he was preparing the large vats. His routine was the same every week. The kitchen would be closed for three hours on

Monday, Wednesday and Friday mornings while he worked on the soup which was always devoured by the insatiable hunger of his clientele before he could obtain the ingredients to repeat the recipe. Soupy was very concerned this particular day because he knew there would be a great demand for his most popular soup over the next few days and there was a good possibility that there would be no more ingredients available for some time. However, that was tomorrow's problem and he refused to let such thoughts interfere with the enjoyment that he always felt in preparing his famous soup.

Sal's barbershop was next to the restaurant and Cindy watched Slug slam the police cruiser to a stop in front of the shop and meander in for a trim. Slug wanted to look good for all of the civilians who would be on hand during the next few days. He knew that a well groomed police officer had a more commanding and authoritative presence.

Sal had been long recognized as the town's most proficient tonsorialist and had been in his present location for over fifteen years. He had two barber chairs for the customers although no one had ever worked with Sal and normally the second chair either was unoccupied or if a large group got together for shop talk, the second chair was as comfortable as the four other chairs which were scattered around the shop. Sal had already cut three heads by the time Slug ambled in and the floor was becoming quite littered with sheared locks. Slim Simms was sitting on the floor doing sit-ups while Sal counted, making sure that Slim's conditioning program was on schedule right up to the day of the big race.

Even though Slim had been a high school star in cross country and was even runner-up in the state meet on two occasions, he had no interest in going to college and only ran in local 10K's and an occasional half marathon. Though he won these with ease, his times were certainly nowhere close to the quality runners who would be coming to town for the marathon on Saturday morning. Several past and future Olympian runners were expected to show for the race. The committee had been able to enlist two major airlines to sponsor prize money of $25,000 for both the winning man and woman runners. As a result elite runners were gathering to try to grab the purse plus test themselves against what would probably be most of the competition for the next Olympics. Slims' best marathon time was over two and one-half hours, but Sal figured that with a little luck and continuing training up to the last minute that Slim might be able to pull off a big upset.

As Slug settled into the chair for his trim, Sal noticed the clown crossing the street to the grassy portion of the courthouse yard. Everyone in town knew that Benny Sardinhurst had his clown ministry for the children during the summers so the policeman and barber paid no attention as the clown proceeded past the window.

However, Cindy was also watching the clown and she put her hand to her mouth. She knew her husband's walk, even with the big shoes and the clown outfit. The painted face wasn't the smiling clown's countenance which was Ben's trademark. It wasn't Benny. Eleanor must have taken one of the clown suits and provided it for Barry. Cindy hoped and prayed that no one else would recognize him.

After Sal finished the trim of Slug, and after making sure that Slim had completed the five-hundred sit-ups, Sal told Slim to take a break and go to Soup's for a seltzer water. Then he locked the door to make sure that no more customers could come in while he made a phone call. He dialed a number in Las Vegas and confirmed to the bookmaker that he was putting all fifty-thousand dollars of the town's remaining funds on Slim Simms to win the marathon on Sunday. The odds were one-thousand to one. After Sal hung up, he washed his sweaty hands and again opened the shop for business. It was a big gamble, and although barbering was his livelihood, gambling was Sal's life, and his nerve endings jumped all through his body after he made the wager.

The bookmaker then called three associates with dark suits and sunglasses and told them to catch the next plane to Iowa and make sure that there would not be a need to pay off the bet.

11

321 Baker Street

Later Wednesday afternoon, Eric arrived in town. He made a quick trip around the town square to see if things had changed over the past few years and then he drove his rented Chevy compact to the Sardinhurst residence, a big two story frame house which was nearly as old as the town. William Sardinhurst had bought the old house just after he and Eleanor got married. Even in his mid-twenties, his ambition was to be mayor of Sam Hill and he thought that this big old house would help him portray the proper image for that political office. He had also envisioned many children in this household, but after watching little Barry go through his antics of childhood and adolescence, he was thankful that Eleanor had convinced him that Barry and Benny would be enough children.

Eric carefully maneuvered around the big mailbox which bore the street number of 321 Baker Street. The drive up the driveway was exhilarating as many memories flashed back through Eric's mind. He glanced across the street and smiled as he saw a horse and buggy hitched to a post in front of the Carlson home. He pulled the car to a stop about even with the back of the house and he could see Benny working on the basket of a hot air balloon in the backyard. As Eric got out of the car, Eleanor came rushing out of the house and gave him a big hug. She told him to come in and see Rachel and Cindy who were preparing supper while his honor, the mayor, was watching the evening news. Benny yelled at Eric to come back out so that he could help with the final design work on the envelope as Benny wanted to use the balloon to preach from during the services Saturday morning for the bikers and marathon runners.

Eleanor took Eric by the hand and led him through the side door and up the short stairway to the kitchen where the younger women were working. Eric figured that between the three women he could catch up on about two years gossip in the next hour. He knew that he would not be able to talk to Cindy about Francesca Johnson or the book about her at this time, but figured that there would be time for this later in the evening. He found an area near the entry to the dining room to stand and not be in the way of the women, but from there he could not see the shadowy figure in odd attire a few feet behind him.

Eleanor told Eric about the troublesome trial at the courthouse and how Mrs. Peck was so afraid that the pressure of the trial would cause the dear judge to put himself into another alcoholic binge. She also mentioned the fact that Sal's mother was very concerned about the possibility that Sal was not acting as a proper fiduciary of the town's funds for the upcoming expenses. The ladies' church group was concerned that he may be misappropriating the money in order to recoup some of his gambling losses. Of course it would be rude to let Valerie know that everyone else was aware of Sal's problems.

Eric looked at the women and thought that these were variations of the stories that he had heard every few years when he returned to town, the only difference being that the women were becoming more matronly in their appearances as the men about whom they worried could not change the flaws in their behavior.

Eric had tried to pay attention to Eleanor who, as the elder spokesperson, had controlled the conversation for the first few minutes. However, his eyes kept darting toward the other women. Cindy had always been comely, but even though they had dated almost exclusively for several years in high school, both had always known that theirs was not to be a life-long relationship.

In fact, Eric had always considered Rachel to be the most beautiful woman he had ever seen. However, she and Barry had always been a pair since grade school and it had always been well known that nothing would come between them. Probably every boy in their class and at least the two classes ahead of them had secretly wanted to go out with Rachel, but it was understood that she was Barry's woman and there is a great deal of honor among the youth in small towns. Besides, theirs was such a relationship that she would never have considered anyone else. Eric kept thinking about this and wondering what would have happened if Barry had been able to stay with Rachel after Zach's death.

Eric finally turned his full attention to Rachel, who had just finished cleaning the vegetables. She was still quite striking even though she was just starting to get locks of gray in her auburn hair. Her eyes still twinkled and her dimples were as deep as when they were in junior high. She appeared to be looking directly through him and it made Eric feel the blood in his veins get heated. She was still working with the patients at Edna's nursing home and he was amazed how she could remain so upbeat with all the problems she had during her life and with the daily chores that she carried on with the elderly and the dying. A slight frown did cross her brow as she mentioned some problems that Carolyn Johnson-Rogers had with Roger Klinker, the young intern who had worked for both Dr. Kellem and Edna. This did not register with Eric until Cindy reminded him that Carolyn was Francesca Johnson's daughter and that Carolyn had also taken a nursing job at Edna's after getting her divorce.

Apparently Carolyn's marriage had been rocky for some time as set forth in the book about Francesca and Robert Kincaid. After the book was published, Carolyn's husband, Charles, felt that the book revealed too many skeletons in Carolyn's family closet and he left town after obtaining a relatively quick divorce. There was some discussion in the county bar association as to whether or not the divorce was legal because judge Peck had slept through the proceedings to prove up the case, but he did sign the papers which the attorneys for Carolyn and her husband drew up.

Rachel's eyes seemed to pierce through Eric to the point where he began to feel very uncomfortable. He remembered seeing that look whenever she was around Barry. He figured that she had been alone for over twenty years now and he was beginning to wonder what might be happening. Then, suddenly, he felt fingers wrapping around his rib cage and he turned to see the clown within inches. He knew that Benny had a clown ministry but wondered how or why Benny would go to the effort of coming in and changing, especially with the balloon not being completely ready.

It was at this exact moment that William Sardinhurst lumbered into the kitchen. He looked at the three women and at Eric and the clown who were in a staring contest and he said, "Well, this looks like some weekend coming up. All of these festivities and my family and friends here to share it with us. What's the matter anyway, Eric? Aren't you going to say hello to Barry?"

12

1963

About a week after the assembly for Barry, William Sardinhurst had called Eric's father. Barry had hitchhiked to California and then caught a ride part way down the Baja where, for several days, he thought about Rachel's condition. Then, as his money became depleted and his hunger increased, he decided it was time to come back home. His father had known that Beauregard Erickson was going to Dallas for a Pepsi Cola convention. Beau was the local Pepsi distributor and attended conventions about once a year. When Barry called his father, William told him to hitchhike back to Dallas where the Erickson's would be in a few days. He could then ride home with them. Beau then told Eric that he could take a few days out of school and go to Dallas for the convention and that they could meet Barry and bring him back home with them.

Although Beau was not terribly interested in politics, his wife, Madeline, was excited about the fact that former vice-president Nixon was to be one of the speakers at the convention. Her joy was compounded when she heard that President Kennedy might possibly also be in the area and she took two extra rolls of film for the new 8 mm camera that Beau had recently purchased.

The Erickson's arrived in Dallas on a Wednesday night and Barry was already in the hotel lobby when they arrived to check in. Barry had forgotten to take extra clothing with him on his journey and Madeline thought that his gray shirt was a little dirty. Barry explained that it was really a white shirt and that indeed it was very dirty. Eric had brought along extra clothing and Barry's letter jacket as the Dallas weather was becoming cool, especially compared to the heat of Mexico. Time has eroded some of the memories from that trip but Eric could later recall that his mother and father had gone to the convention and heard Mr. Nixon speak. His mother also shot a full three minute movie of the former vice-president.

The convention was to continue on through Friday and Beau dutifully went to the convention again. However, Madeline and the boys wanted to see the president and they headed for downtown Dallas. They knew they were running a little late and Madeline decided to put a bandanna over her hair because she didn't have time to put it up that morning. They walked up and down Main Street trying to find a good location to see the president and take a movie, but the crowds were too thick. However, at the end of Main Street and Houston, the crowd seemed to end and there was a nice park area.

Madeline stood in the plaza area on the south side of the road and the boys crossed the street to a location where they could sit at the base of a pergola. The boys could watch the presidential motorcade drive by with very few obstructions. To their right was a man and a woman. He was standing on a small pedestal practicing to take a movie. In front of them near the sidewalk was a couple with two small children and near them were two men, one of whom was carrying an umbrella. They watched Madeline focus her camera directly across the street where she was standing next to a woman without a camera. There were quite a few more people lining the street to the left of the boys and they did hear an ambulance turn on its siren and leave the area just after they got there.

Eric remarked that Madeline was in a position to photograph the president and also have them in the background of her film so that they could prove that they had seen Mr. Kennedy. They didn't even need to look up the street to watch the motorcade as it approached because they could see Madeline fiddling with her camera and aiming it as the motorcade started to pass her. It was at that moment that the shots were ringing out and chaos ensued.

Several minutes later, when the stunned crowd was gathering

around the area where the shooting occurred, Barry went to Madeline and told her to give him the film from the camera. They had no more than taken out the film of the motorcade and replaced it with the film she had taken the previous day at the convention when a man in dark glasses came up and asked to see her camera. He then said that he needed to take the film for analysis for security reasons and he took the film. He said that she should immediately report to an office in the criminal courts building which was directly across the street and that there she would need to give her name and statement as to what she had witnessed.

Barry convinced Eric and Madeline that this was probably not something that they should get involved in and the three of them went back to the hotel where a pledge was taken that no one else, outside of the three of them, should know about the film which Barry would keep and get processed. Madeline was not the type of person to get involved in things which did not concern her and Eric and Barry both believed, after Ruby shot Oswald two days later, that she never mentioned the film to a living soul.

Teenagers being what they are, and especially of the type that these two were, there was a need to involve others and there was a night, the next year, when Eric and Barry were with Rachel and Cindy and a second vow of silence was entered into regarding the film which would clearly show the area of the grassy knoll.

13

BEN

It was well after dark when Bill called everyone into the spacious living room for a family meeting. Ben had worked on the hot air balloon until dark and had not eaten with the rest of the group, but he did grab some leftovers to munch on while the family and extended family gathered. Eleanor had put Eric's suitcase in one of the extra bedrooms and Rachel and Cindy had cleaned up the kitchen. Barry had gone back downtown in the clown suit and when he returned, all seven found chairs and sofas upon which to relax.

Ben watched his father as Bill went from person to person offering snacks to munch on. Bill was a very large man and in his more youthful days projected a powerful image. Neither of the boys had inherited the massiveness of their father, even though both were strongly built and even in middle age maintained excellent fitness. Ever since Ben had been to the seminary, he had likened his father to Saul, the first King of Israel who towered a head above all of the other people. Ben had also considered Barry to be much like Jonathon, the son of Saul who fought the Philistines even against great odds. Even though Ben knew that Bill had flaws and faults like all mortals, Bill was not quick to take credit for accomplishments of others such as Saul had done. At that, Ben decided not to pursue biblical analogies to his family any further.

Ben felt comfortable in his marriage with Cindy and had no sense of jealousy even though Eric had been her high school boyfriend. Eric had been back several times over the years and had often stayed with the Sardinhursts and Ben looked at him more as part of the family than a rival for Cindy's affections. As a matter of fact, shortly after Ben was ordained, Beau and Madeline were killed in a car wreck and one of Ben's first clerical duties was their joint funeral. Ben and Cindy had consoled Eric, and it was then that Ben knew that the relationship between Cindy and Eric was that of close and endearing friendship and not that which lovers and mates would exhibit during trying times.

Eric had asked Ben about the balloon and for several minutes Ben was the center of attention. Everyone but Barry and Eric were fully aware of the balloon project, but nonetheless all respectfully listened while he told the entire group how the balloon was to be used in the furtherance of his ministry.

The plan for Saturday morning was to have a church service at the river about six miles outside of town, next to the Roseman bridge. This would be the campgrounds for the thousands of cyclists who would be coming through town and it would also be about the mid-point of the marathon route. Ben planned to use a megaphone to preach from the balloon at a height where he could be seen from the entire campground. He explained that above the gondola portion of the balloon the skirt would have a Bible verse which would be large enough to be seen from the ground. The main part of the balloon, or the envelope, had a huge crucifix with a rainbow above it representing the New Testament covenant between God and man.

He said that he would need at least one other assistant in the balloon to work the instruments and try to maintain an altitude which would be consistent during the entire worship service. Ben suggested that Eric and Barry might be suitable for this task, but neither seemed too excited about the prospects of controlling a hot air balloon and being forced to listen to Ben give what could be a very long sermon with so many possible souls to reach on the campgrounds below him. However, it would be fun to be in the balloon so they agreed to help.

Rachel was sitting on the floor between the clown's knees. As the conversation shifted to other topics, Ben thought about the horrible night when Cindy told him that Barry and Rachel's son had been killed. Barry had been out running on one of the dirt roads near

Roseman bridge and little Zach was riding along on his bicycle. A car ran Barry off the road and sideswiped the bicycle. Zach had died nearly instantaneously. There had been previous threats to Barry over a film of some kind, but Cindy had never told Ben the particulars about the film and had even asked him not to go into details about it with her. Most people in the town, including his own parents and Rachel's mother, knew generally about the threats and attempt on Barry's life, but the particulars were a secret that apparently belonged only to Cindy, Rachel, Barry and even perhaps Eric since they had all been good friends at about the time of the film incident. The day after Zach's death, and even before the funeral, Barry slipped out of Sam Hill. Only the immediate families knew that Rachel would manage to meet with Barry several times a year at various locations around the country and they would spend long weekends together. Rachel's mother was prone to gossip so she was never told about the occasional rendezvous. It was so painfully obvious to Ben that Rachel and Barry had such a special relationship that the forced long periods of separation was as tragic as any biblical story or fictional tragedy could be. It was good to see them together in his parents home, even though Barry was dressed in one of his clown outfits. Ben realized that the danger to his brother over twenty years earlier was still as real as ever and would remain so as long as the controversy over the film existed. Ben closed his eyes and tried to imagine what could possibly be so important in a piece of film that people would want to kill over it and even more importantly, why wouldn't Barry make some sort of effort to give up the film if this would remove the death threat which was hanging over his head.

Even though Barry was dressed in the clown suit, it seemed such a sad occasion. Rachel had the night shift at Edna's nursing home and it was time for her to go to work. She and Carolyn Johnson-Rogers were the only nurses in town so she needed to pull all of her assigned shifts. Barry wanted to visit with Edna and together, holding hands, he and Rachel said good night to everyone and prepared to leave. As they were walking out the door, Rachel mentioned to

Barry that Roger Klinker, the same young intern at the nursing home who had mistreated Carolyn Johnson-Rogers, braggartly had mentioned that he had been working with Dr. Kellem on a little side business which was very interesting. She told Barry that she wanted to talk to him in greater detail about it on the way to work.

14

THURSDAY

It was hot and humid again. This did not make judge Peck happy as he slipped on the choir robe which had cost him six dollars many years ago when he ascended to the bench. He looked out the window and saw overcast skies which did not pick up his dark mood. He knew that he had a few too many drinks the night before, but he loathed the upcoming trial because of the attention that it would receive and the fact that the spotlight would be on him. All he wanted to do was retire.

In the next room M.L. was studying the list of prospective jurors trying to decide which questions would be appropriate for which witnesses. He had the advantage over the Des Moines lawyer for Dr. Kellem since he was at least friendly toward everyone on the jury list and knew each well enough to call them by their first names.

As the clock outside the courthouse chimed one time indicating it was half-past the hour of nine, the buzzing of the filled courtroom quieted as judge Peck stepped up the steps to his chair above the court reporter's desk and witness seat. The prospective jurors were seated and the judge explained to them the process of voir dire. He then had a temporary respite as the questioning was turned over to the attorneys so that they could ingratiate themselves to the jurors, strike those who seemed to be antagonistic to the cause of the questioner, and hope that the opponent would leave the jurors who appeared most cooperative.

In the back of the spectators' gallery sat Phyllis Noble with her cameras, notepad and purse filled with sharpened pencils. Phyllis was a pretty young thing with snow-white blonde hair that hung straight down her back nearly to her waistline. She had studied journalism arduously and with only one year of college left, she was interning at the local newspaper where her uncle Joe Dermotts was the publisher.

Dermotts and judge Peck had been the best of friends since they both started their respective careers in journalism and law at about the same time. Joe had always seen to it that Frank's name was in the paper whenever possible and Frank had always tipped Joe off on any unusual court filings that were transpiring within the legal realms. They also had been great drinking buddies for the past thirty years. They had even grown alike in their facial features over the year, especially the early morning blood shot eyes and the bulging red veins in their noses from the over indulgences of years past.

Ever since Phyllis came to work early in the summer, Joe had been out of the office more and more. The last two weeks he had been on vacation out of town and Frank deeply regretted not being able to be with his friend and the liquid companionship that they so often shared.

Phyllis was becoming bored with what was obviously going to be a long day of jury-picking. She looked out the window and saw a clown standing on the corner near Soup's Kitchen. Standing just a few yards away from him were three men in black suits and dark glasses who she did not recognize. Even though they were only a few yards away from Sal's barbershop, one of them had binoculars out and was peering through Sal's window. The clown crossed the street and got into a Chevy compact which had a rental company's bumper sticker on it and which had just pulled up and parked. From her vantage point she could also see three other strangers dressed in black with dark glasses who were around the corner from the Soup Kitchen. All three of them had binoculars and were staring intently in the direction of the clown. Phyllis could feel the journalistic juices starting to flow and thought that there might be a better story outside the courtroom than inside on this day. She quietly gathered up her purse and cameras and tiptoed out the back of the courtroom.

Carolyn Johnson-Rogers sat uncomfortably in the jury box.

Although she wanted to be chosen to sit on the jury, she was having trouble paying attention to the questions. She knew that since Dr. Kellem was on trial, his clinic would be closed and Roger Klinker would be trying to pick up extra hours at Edna's since his full-time employer was busy defending himself in the courtroom. Carolyn had tried to avoid Roger as much as possible after the deception he had pulled on her. She felt goosebumps and a cold chill go down her back as she thought about the previous winter.

15

FRANCESCA'S DAUGHTER

The icy wind nearly froze the tears to Carolyn's face as she made a dash to the mailbox. The past week had been uncommonly bad, with the discussions with her mother's biographer, another heated argument with her ex-husband, and notices of past due accounts swelling in the mailbox. Her unemployment compensation had expired and she didn't know if Edna would take her on at the nursing home since she had only recently earned her nursing degree.

Thus, she was quite surprised and in fact quite intrigued to see an envelope quite unlike those to which she was becoming so accustomed.

After throwing the remaining mail on the hutch just inside the doorway, she plopped into her overstuffed chair and opened the letter which appeared to be an invitation. It had no return address on the envelope, but the enclosed card was indeed an invitation. It was from Roger Klinker, a high school classmate who lived a few blocks away but whom she had hardly seen other than at class reunions and occasionally at the grocery store or at one of the social events in Sam Hill. He had interned at Dr. Kellem's clinic and was part-time at Edna's. At first, she thought that the card was an invitation to a party, but upon closer examination, she realized that she was being invited to listen to a reading of short stories which he had written.

Carolyn knew that her strong points did not include decision making. First, she realized she was depressed and felt that it would be too much effort to even consider attending such a function. Next, she hardly knew Roger anymore and certainly had no idea that he was a writer. He had been a decent student and read a lot, but he had always seemed too busy and extroverted to be the type who would sit around and write. Finally, she had too many other things on her mind to worry about and really didn't have the time for such nonsense. She then took the card to the kitchen, crumpled it and dropped it into the paper sack which held the garbage. Then she realized Roger could put in a good word for her at Edna's. She stared at the garbage sack for a few moments and then found herself picking up the phone book to look up Roger's number.

For the next three days, Carolyn could not fully concentrate on her problems. Instead, she was constantly wondering why she had accepted the invitation and what would cause her to do such a foolish thing. These thoughts were still going through her head when she rang the doorbell to Roger's apartment. When Roger opened the door, she realized for the first time that this was not to be a gathering of many people. It would be just the two of them. Her mental frame had been such that she certainly would not have been able to cope with a number of people, but she also knew that she would be very uneasy alone with Roger in his apartment.

He sensed her apprehension as if he could read her mind, and he helped her by making small talk and guiding her around his home. The apartment had every earmark of a man living alone, with organized clutter of books and papers amidst mismatched furniture and wall decor that lacked the grace which most decorators or housewives would provide.

After a few more pleasantries and reminiscences, Roger asked Carolyn if she had any preference for the type of reading that he would do. She was quite surprised by this and told him that he could choose whatever he thought would be suitable.

Roger then took several sheets of paper from a table which supported his typewriter, and he sat in a wicker chair near the sofa where she sat. He cleared his throat and started reading:

"The wind whistled through the valley like the noise of a train approaching a crossing. The air ricocheted off the rocks and drowned the words of the campers who bivouacked far below, near

the foaming waters that raced to no finish line."

Roger looked at Carolyn and paused. Her face was blank, but he sensed that she was already putting aside her daily troubles and was listening to the story. He continued with the reading which lasted nearly half an hour. The words tumbled into sentences and the sentences rolled into paragraphs. The paragraphs blossomed into pages and the pages swept by until the final word. The story was beautiful, even to an untrained critic like Carolyn, and she realized that every sentence had its purpose and this was indeed something special.

After the reading, there was a long silence. It was not discomforting. Carolyn was lost in her own thoughts. She wondered how anyone could write so beautifully. How could this person with whom she had an acquaintance have had such a secret life that no one knew of his artistic gift? These and many other questions crossed her mind. Roger knew what she was thinking and told her that they must not discuss anything further, but if she wanted to return for another story that he would be happy to read to her.

Carolyn returned the following weekend and Roger read to her and again, the flow of the story was perfect. The continuity was easy to ascertain. His grammar and syntax were flawless. Similes and metaphors abounded throughout the reading. It was like nothing she had ever heard.

At the end of the second reading, he told her that they must maintain two rules. They would not discuss the meaning of his works since he was only the author and not a critic and she must never ask him personal questions about the writings.

Sometime between the second reading and the fourth, it became obvious to Carolyn that she was becoming very distracted by these stories and her curiosity about Roger left her spending endless hours fantasizing over the mystery behind his talent.

One day Carolyn realized that she had attended 16 readings with Roger and she was now listening to two stories a week. But even more surprising, she realized that the winter had passed and a full season was behind her from the time she had first received his invitation. She had known more than 120 seasons, but she felt that her life had finally turned around during this last winter.

The spring passed quickly and she could hardly wait for the evenings when Roger would read to her. The stories were all so beautiful. She realized that his stories were not only perfect in the form of construction, but were beautiful in theme. The themes would gravitate toward the highest potential for humanity, and the protagonist would always emerge victorious, even in recognizing and contending with the sufferings and disheartening realities of the less noble aspects of life.

After one especially wonderful reading, she told Roger that his stories had helped her out of her depression. He suggested that perhaps the facts that she had obtained employment at Edna's and was more at ease with the publication of the book about her mother and Kincaid might have something to do with it. She felt a sense of self-confidence that she had not known for many years and then realized she was falling in love with Roger. She told Roger she wanted to talk to him about the meaning of the stories and about his motivation for writing. He then told her that she had broken the rules and he could not continue either with the conversation or with any further readings.

The next morning Carolyn felt that she should buy a gift for Roger to show her gratitude and hopefully mollify him for being upset with her for speaking about things which were against his rules.

During her lunch break she drove to the library. She asked Cynthia if there were any excellent books of short stories which she could give as a present to Roger. Cindy told her that over the past few months Roger had checked out almost every good book of short stories that she had in stock. However, there was one book that Roger may have missed. Within a few minutes, the book was in Carolyn's hand. Carolyn started leafing through the book to try to determine which of the stories were worthy of Roger. Suddenly, her body turned cold and her extremities became numb as her eyes fixed on the words at the top of the page: "The wind whistled through the valley like the noise of a train ...."

16

LET'S MAKE A DEAL

Eric had seen Barry in front of the barbershop and pulled his little rental car into the only open space on the block surrounding the courthouse. Barry quickly crossed the street and slid into the passenger's seat. Neither of them could immediately figure out why the Washington people would be so bold as to come up and stand next to Barry in broad daylight and on the main street in town. They watched the three men in the rear view mirror and became even more perplexed as it became apparent that the men were focusing their attention on the barbershop.

Then, to add further mystery to the strange situation, the back door of the car opened and a young girl with several cameras and a notebook and large purse plopped down on the back seat. There was a short eternity of silence as she rolled down the rear door's window in an effort to obtain a small amount of movement of air in what was already becoming a hot August day.

Phyllis immediately got to the point. "I'm Phyllis Noble, and I work at the newspaper. My uncle is Joe Dermotts and over the years I have heard every story about everyone who ever set foot in this town. I assume that you are Eric Erickson and my hunch is that your buddy is not our town clown and minister extraordinaire, but rather his brother, the long lost Barry Sardinhurst."

The next silence was slightly longer than the first.

She continued, "I have just seen at least six strangers sneaking around this town with dark suits, binoculars and sunglasses."

She stared at Barry. "Everyone in town knows that you have been in hiding ever since your little boy was killed out by Roseman bridge. The rumors and speculations have been from one extreme to the other. Some folks think that it may have even had something to do with the accident which claimed the lives of your friend's parents."

Eric turned his head full to get a good look at her and saw that she had rolled her eyes in his direction when she mentioned his parents.

She studied them both for another moment and then continued, "We may be putting out an extra edition of the paper over the week-end because of all the events that are planned. I don't imagine you gentlemen would be too particularly pleased to see an item in the paper that the mayor's oldest son is in town visiting. As a matter of fact, I probably could even get out one of our file pictures of Ben running around town in that silly clown suit handing out candy to the children with wrappers containing Bible verses, and then let all of our readers know who the clown really is. I am sure that if the half dozen Blues Brothers who are within ear-shout of us haven't figured you out yet, they will be able to read."

Eric and Barry stared at each other, trying to read each other's minds and think of some response to Phyllis. While they were contemplating this, several boys who had not yet reached their teens came running by the car and one of them slowed down and yelled at Barry, "Hey, preacher man, throw us some candy but stick the wrap-pers up your butt."[2]

Barry turned back to Phyllis and said, "You sure have everything pegged, right down to the last Bible verse."

A large smile came over her face and she said, "Not only that, but that kid would not have even been here to talk his trash except for something that you did many years ago. That was Slug Marshall's grandchild. It was his father that you pulled out of the cob fire, or at least that's what people say."

Barry could see a chink in her armor and thought that she might not be so tough to deal with. He said, "Look, I'm sure you think that the little scenario you just suggested would be a fun story to write and you would be getting a scoop of sorts. However, nobody is that concerned now as to when and if a relic from the past happens to stumble through town. I think there may be a story or two in the making that could be much more beneficial to your journalistic talents and if you promise to put any mention of me on the back burner, perhaps we can work together to give your readers something of a bit more substance. How about making a deal?"

She raised an eyebrow and said to Barry, "I'm sure your bluffing, Sardinhurst. I doubt if you have any story that you have picked up in the last few hours or day that you have been in town that can top anything that I have been working on while snooping around this town my entire life. I may have been born at night, but I wasn't born last night."

Barry recognized that she was going to be pretty tough to deal with, but perhaps he could use the situation to his advantage. He decided to open from another direction. "Look, Phyllis, you put off any mention of me in the extra and I will not only help get you better stories, but I want you to work with me to develop these stories so that you can be there and get first hand information to take to press. That way if I'm not giving you anything of value, you can always insert your findings about me at the last minute."

She thought about this for a second. Then, as her eyes shifted from the clown to the driver as she spoke, she said, "I will go along with your suggestion on one more condition. I want to know the whole story as to why you disappeared after your son's death and whether it had anything to do with the car wreck involving the Ericksons."

The summer's heat was beginning to make the paint on the clown's face run and it appeared that tears were starting to roll down his cheeks. It was then agreed that she would take no notes but could listen as the two men recalled other events from another time.

Barry told Eric to drive slowly to Edna's nursing home and on the way they told Phyllis that she could become privy to that minute part of the history of Sam Hill which had hitherto been a secret between Eric, Cindy, Barry, and Rachel.

As they left the courthouse square and headed toward Edna's, they went by a dozen motorcyclists who were heading into the downtown area. They were all driving big choppers with their molls pulling tight on their leather jackets as the engines roared.

Slug was sitting with his feet on his desk when he heard the cycles several blocks away. He rubbed his clean cut hairline and mumbled to himself, "Looks like I'm going to have to start earning my money now."

[2] All three people in the car have filed sworn statements that this was the very language used by the town cops' grandson. Since the comment was made outside the car, it was not picked up on the recorder Phyllis had in her purse. All the other quotes in this chapter were on the tape she was recording while in the car.

<h1 style="text-align:center">17</h1>

<h2 style="text-align:center">1965</h2>

Barry and Rachel had married over the semester break of their high school senior year. In those days, girls did not finish high school when they got married. There was a rule forbidding pregnant girls from going to school and consequently this meant that all married girls were required to quit. Rachel would ultimately go back and get her GED and then attend a nursing school, but that was after Zach's death. Meanwhile, in what would have otherwise been her senior year, she stayed home, barefoot and pregnant.

Barry picked up a couple part-time jobs while he was finishing school and after Zach was born the next summer, he did attend the local community college, which was then called a junior college. The film from Dallas was given to Barry since Madeline did not want to get involved and Eric trusted Barry to take care of it.

The boys had heard stories of strange deaths to the witnesses in Dallas and became even more reluctant to share their story with anyone. They knew no one that they could trust to even develop the film for them.

After the Warren Commission came out with its findings in the fall of 1964, books started appearing which suggested how Oswald may not have acted alone and it became more frighteningly apparent to the young men that Madeline's film may have shown evidence which would have changed the historic analysis of the assassination.

If they tried to turn the film over to the authorities, they would be identified as witnesses to the shooting and might suffer the same fate as others who were believed to have seen something contrary to the official version.

Rachel was busy caring for the baby but at that time Cindy had started working full time at the library. Barry and Eric hoped that perhaps she might be able to help locate someone who could be trusted to develop the film. Cindy used the resource materials available at the library, and after several months of worry and thoughtful meditation about this problem, she finally came up with a solution that seemed workable.

She had been stacking periodicals one day when she found a story in *National Geographic* which attracted her attention to the problem of the film. A writer for the magazine had travelled to Dallas and done an article about Dealey Plaza and how it was attracting tourists much like a shrine. The back page of the magazine showed a picture of the author and the photographer who accompanied him. The photographer's name was Robert Kincaid and he looked quite a bit like a hippie. Barry and Eric agreed with Cindy that this long-haired back-packer was probably quite independent from any authorities or government people who might make things unpleasant for their withholding of evidence.

The main headquarters for the *National Geographic* did have a home listing for Kincaid. However, since he was gone on assignment all over the world for such long periods of time, it was nearly another year before he could be reached at his home in the Northwest. Barry and Eric had each tried at least twice a week to call him and had even double checked his number several times through his employer.

When Barry finally reached him, he explained to Kincaid that they had seen his photograph in the magazine and felt that he could be trusted to develop a very important film for them. Kincaid politely responded that he was very busy and without the blessings of his employer, he doubted if he would be able to make a side trip to Iowa in the near future. Barry then told him the story of Dealey Plaza and that the film might contain frames which could prove or disprove existence of a shooter in the area that was being referred to as the grassy knoll in the newly published literature. Kincaid was definitely interested in the film after hearing Barry's story. However, he needed a reason to convince his employers to allow him time to come to Iowa. It was then that Barry suggested a feature on the seven bridges of Madison county which were all about a century old.

Within another ten days, arrangements were made for Kincaid to come to Iowa and shoot pictures of the covered bridges. It was agreed that Eric, Barry and Cindy would meet with Kincaid at the Roseman bridge the night he got in town. However, in his excitement, Kincaid lost the directions and he happened to stop at Francesca Johnson's house for directions. Her husband and the kids were off showing some of the livestock that week and even though Francesca had been a faithful wife up to that point, her Italian bloodlines prevailed when she met Kincaid and the innocent farm wife became instantly distracted by the ponytailed photographer from the West.

Barry, Eric and Cindy had been waiting for Kincaid by the Roseman bridge as planned. They were aghast when they saw Kincaid pull up in a rented vehicle with Francesca Johnson sitting in the cab next to him. They hid in the bushes just below the bridge while he set up and took photographs while she watched.

Robert and Francesca finally left about supper time and it was nearly two hours later before Kincaid finally returned. He explained that she came with him just to give him directions and that he could not get rid of her. About this time they saw Francesca's car pulling to the other side of the bridge and again they all hid, this time Kincaid was with them. Francesca got out and put a note in one of the loose planks on the edge of the bridge and she left. The old bridge did have plenty of holes in it since the county had not had the funds to keep the bridges up and the holes in the sides and top of the covered bridges continued to grow each year.

Kincaid had obviously become preoccupied with Francesca and the interest he had initially shown for the film was diminishing. However, Kincaid did agree to meet them two days later at the local newspaper. He had written a letter of introduction to Joe Dermotts, the new publisher of the paper and Dermotts had promised him he could use the dark room for his photographic work while he was in the area. In exchange Dermotts wanted to do a story about Kincaid.

Kincaid's preoccupation became an obsession over the next ninety-six hours and he kept delaying the meeting to develop the film. Finally, on the last afternoon before he left town, he did meet with Barry and Eric at the newspaper. They had noticed that the Johnson family had returned from their trip and it was quite obvious why Kincaid had been unavailable until that time.

Kincaid took Barry and Eric into the dark room with him and Barry handed a small roll of film to Kincaid. Just as the processing was nearly completed, the door to the dark room opened and light shined upon the developing film. Dermotts and his friend, the newly appointed judge Peck, had been celebrating Peck's appointment and Peck thought he was walking into the bathroom. Shortly thereafter, Kincaid left town and was never again seen by any Sam Hillian.[3]

About one year later, certain researchers in the nation's capital were going through movies and still photographs taken in Dealey Plaza and they came across several pictures which showed two young boys, one of whom was wearing a letter jacket. Filed reports indicated that these two young men had been seen in the company of a woman whose film had obviously been switched.

Within a few more days the manufacturer of the letter jacket verified the school which had ordered it and not much later, identities were made on the two young boys and the woman with the bandanna and the camera.

---

[3] No exact quotes have been used in this chapter. Although Phyllis captured the earlier dialogue in the car on her recorder, the battery died just as Barry and Eric began telling her the story of Kincaid.

18

EDNA'S RETIREMENT HOME

Phyllis had left her sharpened pencils in her purse as she had promised while she listened to the story of the film. She asked Barry and Eric why they had never notified the authorities that the film had been destroyed. They told her that there had been efforts to convey such a message, but the first problem was trying to determine who they needed to convince that the film was of no value. Obviously someone wanted the film very badly and it was quite probable that Beauregard and Madelines' deaths were no accident when their car went over the embankment at Miller's Curve, a road that they had known and driven all of their adult lives. Also, Barry was convinced it was no accident that he was run off the road and Zach was hit and killed by the hit and run driver.

Whoever wanted the film would certainly not believe it was destroyed and Barry told Phyllis that over the years, while he had been on the run, he had had several close calls. Now, Kincaid had been dead for several years and judge Peck had been too drunk to even realize where he was when he allowed the light to be shed upon the film. Phyllis was still pondering this matter when they drove around to the back of Edna's home.

Edna had always made things as comfortable as possible for her patients and retirees. Behind the home, she had a wooded area for walking and various entertainment sites such as a softball field, a small dog track where Sal would be the head handicapper on the weekends and of course the pond.

Rachel was off duty but she was down at the pond helping strap some of the stroke victims into the modified golf carts. The dimensions in length and width of the pond were nearly identical to that of the old cob pile. The pond itself was very shallow except for an area of about forty feet in the middle where there was a big drop off and the better fishermen among the retirees could drop a line where the well stocked catfish, bluegills and an occasional northern pike would snap at the bait. The remaining portion of the pond was so shallow that the residents could use it as a wading pool and it would be safe for the golf carts that would get bumped into the pond. An asphalt path ran all the way around the pond and was just wide enough for two carts to go abreast. Those residents and patients who were unable to drive would be strapped into the passenger side of the cart while the more able-bodied persons would be the drivers.

Edna's official rules were that everyone was to drive slowly around the path and to pass only on the right with a limit of six carts on the path at one time. However, no one obeyed the rules and in fact it was great fun for everyone to use the cart path as a raceway. Every night, the main topic of conversation in Edna's dining room was not the expected discussion of maladies and misadjustments of physical parts in the old and failing bodies, but instead it would run along the lines of drivers who were best able to force the most other carts into the pond. Glass-eyed Vincent Schumacher at age eighty-four was still too coordinated for anyone else in the home and he held both the daily and weekly record for most pond carts with four and twenty-three respectively. There was usually a rush after breakfast to get to the front of the line to have the privilege of being co-pilot with the one- eyed man.

Eric and Barry helped Rachel towel off a few of the unfortunate drivers and passengers who got in the way of Glass-eye and as soon as a couple aides came to relieve Rachel, they went inside to talk to Edna. Phyllis stayed outside snapping pictures of the carts smashing into each other, thinking that she might be able to develop this into a human interest story.

About forty-five minutes later, Edna put down her coffee cup and stood up from behind her desk in her spacious private office. She looked slowly around the room, first looking at Eric, then at Rachel and finally at Barry in the clown's outfit. She looked out the window and saw Phyllis still taking pictures and on the other side of the pond in the wooded area she could see Slim Simms running barefoot in the woods in a final conditioning effort for the big race now only a day and a half away. She picked up the phone and dialed a number from her rolodex. She said, "Slug, I know you still have a key to every business in town so that you can check them at night for intruders. I want you to stop out here this afternoon and bring your keys with you."

19

SUPPERTIME

Carolyn was left on the jury. By late afternoon, the jury selection had been completed as were the opening statements. Judge Peck had allowed everyone to go home early stating that the first witnesses would be presented by Mr. Ullestad bright and early Friday morning.

Slug had sensed that the judge would drag his feet on this trial as long as possible to insure it would be the last thing that he did before retirement. Accordingly, Slug was waiting for Ullestad in his office in the middle of the afternoon. He was concerned about the motorcycle gang that was descending upon the town and wanted to know if there were any city ordinances that could be prevailed upon to use as leverage to chase the cyclists out of town until the weekend festivities were over. He hoped to at least encourage them to pack up and continue on up to Sturgis, South Dakota, where the annual motorcycle rally was being held the next week. Ullestad searched through the state and municipal codes but could find nothing to help Slug. There were some noise ordinances but Slug new that these rough looking motorcyclists would probably take offense at such a minor misdemeanor. It would be better to do nothing than try to start filing such petty charges.

It was nearly suppertime when Slug remembered that he promised Edna that he would drop by and bring his set of keys. As he walked out the courthouse into the blistering summer air, he noticed Sal locking up the barbershop and heading toward Soup's for supper.

As Slug started to back up the mauve and green police car, he glanced in the rearview mirror and noticed three men dressed in black suits with sunglasses who all seemed to be staring in the direction of the restaurant through binoculars. Slug wondered why these strangers were wearing such dark clothing in the heat of the summer and figured they must be vacationers who didn't know how to dress for the Iowa heat.

Looking at his watch, he realized he was running late so he turned on the siren and squealed around the corner of the square as he headed toward the retirement home. It was a good thing that he had turned on the siren or he would have smashed into Soupy, who was just pulling out of the alley behind his restaurant. Soupy was in his stationwagon with several empty containers which needed to be filled with his special formula.

At Edna's, things appeared to be going on a routine for late Thursday afternoon. The go-cart races were over and those who were able to drive themselves had done so. The invalids had been unharnessed from the passenger's seats and dried off and brought back to the main lodge area. Most of the others had returned to the lake for the Thursday night fish contest. Every Friday was fish day and whoever caught the most fish would be the person who got to call out the numbers at Bingo on both Friday and Saturday nights. Eric and Phyllis had stayed to officiate the weighing of the fish and also insure that there would be no fisticuffs among the fishermen who managed to tangle their lines with each other.

Barry and Edna had continued to converse alone throughout the afternoon while Rachel kept an eye on Roger Klinker, who spent most of the afternoon in the kitchen listening to the local radio station. When it was announced that the trial had adjourned early for the day, Roger clocked out and left. He was just leaving the parking lot as Slug came roaring in.

As Slug walked up the sidewalk to the front door of the nursing home, he feared that the stress of his job was causing him to lose a grip on reality. He knew that he had just seen the three strangers with their black suits and dark glasses in town as he was leaving the courthouse square, but here they were again standing behind the bushes peeping in Edna's office window.

<h1 style="text-align:center">20</h1>

A SCOOP FOR PHYLLIS

Edna convinced Slug that by leaving a couple keys he would be repaying an old debt and she assured him that nothing would be taken from the business owners whose doors could be unlocked with the keys. Slug had known Edna for nearly fifty years and knew that she could be trusted and that she influenced a great many votes each time he had to run for office. Even though he was not completely comfortable with giving the keys to Edna, he figured that going along with her was probably better than incurring her anger.

After Slug left, Edna handed the keys to the clown who rounded up Eric and Phyllis. Since Roger had snuck out, Edna was again short on help so Rachel volunteered to work the night shift.

The sun was setting as Eric maneuvered the rental car out of the parking area and headed down the road toward the Kellem Clinic.

As they neared the clinic they saw two cars and a station wagon parked behind the single story building. The only light in the building was from one of the rooms toward the back of the building. Eric turned off the lights on the car and, after shifting it into neutral, let it coast across the street where he came to a stop. Phyllis was decked out with several cameras and led the way. Barry had removed the oversized shoes which were part of the clown's outfit, but the remainder of the suit was intact. Eric followed Barry as the three silently crossed the street. Following the shadows they crept slowly to the front door which opened noiselessly after Phyllis inserted Slug's key.

The next half-hour seemed an eternity as they crept and crawled from room to room until the voices which were far away at first became distinct and clear. Kneeling outside the door which kept them from being seen by the three persons in the other room, Phyllis could see through the door's window what the three were doing. She took out her best indoor camera, adjusted the shutter speed and fired off all the film that she had with her. Then she, Eric and the clown backtracked out of the building and proceeded to the dark room in the newspaper building.

Judge Peck had retired to his couch in the game room of his home and was blissfully sleeping with his empty Southern Comfort bottle resting on his chest. This time he was not in a position to interfere with the processing and the film could be, without his intervention, developed.

21

FRIDAY MORNING

By the time judge Peck was ready for trial, it was nearly 10:00 a.m. Not only did he leave home late for the courthouse, but for the first time in the history of Sam Hill, there was a traffic jam building in the downtown area. There were nearly three hundred motorcyclists and most were circling the courthouse square looking for their friends and acquaintances from previous cycling events.

Also, many of the runners had arrived in town and were trying to acclimate themselves to the heat which was again pushing the thermometer well over eighty degrees before mid-morning. Most of them were still breaking in their marathon shoes. They were doing various stretching exercises, walking, jogging, and in general creating quite a nuisance for the vehicle traffic, all to the disdain of Slug and his two deputies.

The only relief from the already scorching sun was a small shadow cast by the hot air balloon which slowly circled the town square. The bright colors of the rainbow had been finished and the balloon was a most impressive sight, especially when it was lowered to a point where the biblical verse was viewable to the potential congregation which was amassing around the courthouse.

Ullestad had time to present two preliminary witnesses to the jury during the morning session of Kellem's trial. The first witness was the state medical examiner who described to the jury the structure of a fetus during various periods from conception to viability and eventually through birth. Next, the head of the state medical board testified that the medical definition of life was not necessarily at odds with the theological concept that prevailed among most fundamental preaching. Carolyn and the other eleven chosen jurors listened intently, in spite of the distractions caused by the heat and noises from outside the courthouse which managed to penetrate the old building. As Carolyn listened to the testimony, she felt a concern for the health problems of the community as she began to realize that if Kellem were to be convicted, his license would be stripped and at present the only other potential provider of medical care would be Roger Klinker. Most people realized that Klinker was much too much like Kellem and if he ever did receive his license after the internship, he would eventually lose it and anyway, people would be very reluctant to go to him.

At the same time the Dorcas Society was having a final meeting in the church basement. The same heavy thoughts seemed to be on their minds and they prayed that another doctor could be found to provide for the health needs of the town. They continued their petitions for Sal, the judge, and for Slug. Eleanor also took Marie aside and shared with her the fact that Rachel had been seeing Barry on occasion over the years. Even though Marie had never accepted Barry because of the shame that he had cast upon the Witherspoon family by the impregnation of Rachel, she finally started to realize that Rachel's source of happiness was Barry. The last item of business for the members of the Dorcas Society concerned the race,and Edna, who was able to attend the meeting because Rachel volunteered to stay and work the morning shift, spent about one-half hour quietly discussing what needed to be done the next day.

Soupy was through with his formula early in the morning since he knew there would be a huge crowd in the restaurant for the next two days. As part of his marketing technique, he opened the doors to the restaurant and turned on several fans to blow the aroma of his famous cuisine into the street and beyond. These aromas filtered through the courthouse building and by 11:30 the stomachs of the jurors, witnesses, attorneys and judge were all growling so loud that it was impossible to hear the testimony. Judge Peck then excused the jury for lunch and instructed his bailiff to escort the jurors to Soup's for a well deserved lunch, compliments of the state judiciary fund.

By 11:45 the twelve jurors were seated at a large round table in the middle of the dining room. Three men in sunglasses were just finishing their soup from the corner booth from which they could keep an eye on Sal's barbershop. At exactly 12:00 the famous luncheon special soup was being devoured by the hungry jurors. They knew that the reputation of this fine meal was that it not only tasted good, but actually made people feel younger and improved their complexions. Exactly two minutes later Phyllis, Eric, and a clown entered the restaurant and used the key to the front door to lock everyone in. Phyllis then announced that she had some pictures to show the jurors and she wanted to interview them for a special edition of the paper which would be coming out early the next week.

As this was transpiring, three more men wearing sunglasses and dark suits pushed their noses against the glass of the locked door, squinting in an effort to see what was going on.

22

A SCOOP OF SOUP

The clown was carrying a briefcase filled with the photos that had been taken the night before. Phyllis and Eric started placing the photographs on the large round table where the jurors sat. When she noticed that the men with the dark suits and sunglasses had also been devouring the famous soup, Phyllis made sure that several photographs were also placed on their table.

The jurors silently looked at the photographs and passed them from person to person. The men in the sunglasses peered over the top of their spectacles and slowly as the implications from the pictures began to be grasped by the viewers, each and every one became ashen and a sense of community nausea enveloped the area.

The first photos clearly showed Dr. Kellem, Roger Klinker and Soupy Campbell pouring the product of Dr. Kellem's abortion work into Soupy's special formula bottles. Others showed the three men using equipment in the clinic to liquefy all of the aborted material to the point that it was no thicker than salsa dip. Another grouping of pictures showed Soupy putting the material into a blender where the remaining chunks of bone and clot were pulverized and blended into the rich liquid which would ultimately become the secret ingredient for which people would travel hundreds of miles to taste.

Once the diners comprehended the meaning of the photographs, their reactions varied. Two of the jurors got immediately sick and vomited on the table, floor, and whoever was within range of their regurgitations. Several others went into immediate denial in an effort to avoid similar physical cleansing. Carolyn Johnson-Rogers confirmed in her own mind that Roger Klinker was even worse than Dr. Kellem or Soupy, because Klinker not only enjoyed this grotesque game that was being played out among the unsuspecting diners at the restaurant, but he also relished in the mental abuse involving the cruel hoax he had played upon her. As she watched her fellow jurors pass from denial to acceptance, with the physical retching that came with it, Carolyn could do no more than weep.

The three men in the corner booth were not better off than the others after they realized what they had been eating. Even though each of them in the past had on occasion broken a few fingers and noses as a part of their livelihood, this particular perversion was of a deeper dimension than any of them had ever experienced. Like most of the jurors, they found themselves uncontrollably gagging and hoping that they could completely empty their stomachs of that substance which but a few minutes ago was thought to be the best soup of which they had ever partaken.

Phyllis was patiently waiting for the physical effects of the pictures to run its toll so that she could start the interview process. However, she heard the sound of breaking glass and turned toward the door just in time to see three men in dark suits and sunglasses toss canisters of tear gas into the room. In a moment, what had previously been a chaotic situation became complete panic as all of the customers rose and while attempting to fight back both tears and the continuing urge to puke, made for the doorway and the outside environment.

The three men from the outside were convinced that the pictures had something to do with a small grassy area in Texas in 1963. They grabbed most of the photos and scampered through the broken door and headed back across the street to the courthouse square. The motorcyclists and the runners, who had all maintained a distance, but had seen the breaking of the glass and the tear gas attack, surrounded the escaping men with the photographs.

Slug and his two deputies, who had been directing traffic, arrived within seconds and took the three men to the jail cell in the courthouse. Slug tried to find Soupy to see if he wanted to file charges for the damage to the restaurant, but several witnesses said they saw

Soupy's stationwagon heading out of town immediately after the fiasco at the restaurant. Phyllis, who wanted her photographs returned, requested a few moments of private conversation with these men, which Slug granted.

Phyllis told the three men that the film they were looking for was destroyed many years earlier and their investigation must immediately cease. If not, she would publish a story about the strange circumstances of the deaths of Madeline and Beau Erickson and little Zack Sardinhurst. This would not be good publicity for their employer whose image was already tarnished by a suspicious public. She then gathered up all the photos and on the way out she told Slug that she did not want to press any charges for attempting to steal the pictures. She also suggested that he probably should release the three prisoners.

By mid-afternoon, those jurors who had recovered enough to report back to the courthouse were excused. Judge Peck had immediately declared a mistrial after learning of the out of court revelations to the jurors who could not possibly be impartial any longer. At first Peck had been quite irritated by what had happened, but after a short consideration he realized how fortunate things had worked out since he could quite easily postpone any new trial against Kellem until such time as he was safely retired. He then grabbed a pint of whiskey from the office safe in his chambers and went whistling out of the courthouse knowing that he could quench his thirst as he would drive slowly home.

As Peck took his first big swig at the stop sign three blocks from the courthouse, he paused to wait for the ambulance which came roaring around him with its siren going and the lights flashing. Slug was the volunteer emergency driver and the judge could see Slug grinning childishly as he sped through the intersection.

Peck knew that Kellem's lawyer had advised the doctor to leave town until the next trial was scheduled to start, but he was puzzled as to why the ambulance would be heading toward Des Moines when it could have taken its victim to the clinic where Roger Klinker would handle things temporarily.

What the judge did not know was that the victim in the ambulance was Roger Klinker. He had been alone in the alley behind Soup's restaurant about an hour earlier retrieving the remaining vats of ingredients so that they could be sold to a restauranteur in Des Moines.

Unfortunately for Klinker, an angry clown saw him there. While Eric stood guard at the corner of the alley for the next three minutes, Klinker became painfully aware that his assistance in developing the fetal residue into a delicacy was unacceptable. Perhaps even worse was his offensive behavior toward Carolyn Johnson-Rogers at a time when she was most vulnerable. After receiving both a tongue lashing and a thorough physical beating, Klinker felt the remainder of the warm special ingredients being poured all over him. His tongue found a couple of empty spaces where his teeth had been and through his swollen eyes he could see the clown cross the street and go to the pay phone booth from which the ambulance was summoned. The last thing Roger remembered before waking up in a body cast at the hospital was the sweet taste of the ingredient dripping into the new spaces in his mouth.

23

FRIDAY NIGHT

Early in the afternoon, there was concensus at Sal's that it was best for Sam Hill that the Kellem trial was at least temporarily behind them. Most of the men who came into Sal's later in the day were there to pay off Sal.

Several weeks before the trial started there was speculation that there would be a huge crowd of demonstrators both for and against abortion during the trial. Sal had taken the position, with generous odds, that there would be absolutely no demonstrations. After all the bets were made, he made sure that the motorcycle clubs throughout Iowa, Kansas, Missouri and southern Illinois were all aware of the festivities which were timed to run concurrently with the trial. Since the bikers were to be gathering for their annual trek to the Badlands, Sal invited them to Sam Hill as their first meeting place.

The fact that several hundred motorcyclists would be in Sam Hill was a deterrent to both the pro and anti-abortion sides, which always seemed to relish confrontation with each other. However, they were more than slightly intimidated by the possibility of meeting motorcyclists who might be on the opposing side of their issue. Thus, neither side of the abortion demonstration fanatics showed for the trial. Under the terms of the bet, the mistrial instituted conclusion of the wager and Sal delighted in the quarters and dollars that poured in throughout the afternoon.

As Sal locked the door after collecting his last winning, he told Slim to make sure that he attended the carbohydrate loading spaghetti supper at Edna's and to get a good night's rest since the race was to start at 7:00 sharp the next morning. As Slim jogged down the street and turned the corner to head toward Edna's, a sweat broke out over Sal's entire body. He realized that he had gotten himself in too deep this time and he wondered how he would be explaining to the town's people in a few days that their funds were lost on an impossible gamble that he had taken.

Edna had several tents set up for the spaghetti supper. The Friday fish luncheon had ended early and Edna had spent the afternoon with several patients and members of the Dorcas Society who had forgotten what they had talked about earlier that morning. Since Roger had not returned to work, Edna had asked Rachel to stay on throughout the day to help set up the tents for dishing out the spaghetti. Rachel knew that this was going to be a lot of extra work so she also volunteered to stay over Friday night to help start putting everything away.

Several members of the motorcycle gangs had volunteered to help serve the runners the traditional carbo loading meal and Edna promised all the helpers that they could eat free once the runners were done. Word spread quickly and by the time the first runners arrived at 6:00 p.m., over four hundred motorcycles were parked in line along the curbing that ran from Edna's front door clear out to the main road and four blocks back into the town area.

Runners were sporting their racing t-shirts from far and famous places signifying to any interested people that these hardened soldiers of the foothills and roads were experienced harriers who were prepared for the 26.2 mile grind of the next day.

As the crowd increased, the excitement for the next day's festivities could not be contained, and the runners, motorcyclists, townspeople and residents could all feel the uncontainable excitement which was filling the air.

The excitement could even be felt inside the balloon which was being given its final test run over the crowd before returning to town and descending behind 321 Baker Street.

24

THE RACE

Most Saturday mornings in Sam Hill are quiet and movement by the citizens is slow to creeping. However, this was no typical Saturday morning and there was hustling and bustling even before dawn. Old Sol seemed confused by the break in the routine and the normal brilliant sunlight was hidden by a cloud cover which prevailed for the first time in several weeks. But even the cloud cover could not hide the humidity and temperature from skyrocketing into the low eighties by six a.m.

By that time, the runners were stretching and jogging and loosening their muscles. A last minute contingent of eighty runners from the Capitol Striders in Des Moines moved the total number in the field to be in excess of four thousand. The volunteers from the Dorcas Society had been working at the water and aid stations for over an hour filling cups with water and gatorade at each three mile marker.

Several trainers had measured the distance of the course to insure it was the exact twenty-six miles three-hundred and eighty-five yards. The start line was at the northeast corner of the courthouse and the gigantic loop would finish on the southeast corner of the courthouse. The half marathon mark was where the main highway met the gravel road which was only two blocks from the Roseman bridge. The deacons, elders and most of the parishioners from Benny's church were setting up the revival tent and chairs and benches on the hillside just off the nearly empty creek bed which ran under the Roseman bridge. It was anticipated that many of the runners would stop at the half-way mark because of the heat and the fact that not many of the mid-pack runners were well prepared for a marathon in August. Those runners, along with the motorcyclists who had camped in the area, would be the prime targets for the revival.

While these activities were going on, Sal was giving Slim a final rub down on the floor of the barbershop. There was no room on the courthouse yard because of all the other runners, helpers, spectators, and the motorcyclists who were scratching their beards wondering why any sane person would be anxious to run such a distance, especially at a time of day when most people should be getting ready to go to bed. As Sal was applying the vaseline and balm to Slim's extremities, three men in dark suits and wearing sunglasses were conferring a few feet away from the front entrance to the barbershop.

At a few minutes before 7:00, Slug positioned the police car in front of the starting line where he was to be the pace car driver for the leaders. A couple photographers from Des Moines were allowed to sit on the trunk of his vehicle so they could take pictures of the front runners. Slug was a little nervous since he had not driven within the speed limit for several years and did not know if he would be able to touch the accelerator lightly enough to do his assignment. As he turned on the siren to call the runners into position, there was a flurry of activity as the elite and faster runners jockeyed for position near the front. Even though the street had been cleared of parking for the race, it was not wide enough to accommodate such a huge mass of runners who completely filled the street from the starting line back to the finish line.

As the runners were nervously checking their watches and jumping up and down to release some of the pent up adrenaline, a clown appeared at the front with a megaphone. He told the runners to make sure that the best runners were at the front and announced that the race would begin in three minutes.

At the same time, Eric, who was an expert at handing out literature, with the help of Phyllis, started handing out brochures to all of the runners at the front. The brochures were announcing another marathon which would be run the next weekend in Des Moines through the sponsorship of the Capitol Striders running club. Since most of the best runners were of foreign extract, the brochures were printed not only in English, but also in Spanish, French, Italian, German, Dutch, Russian, Greek, Indian, and in various dialects for the Kenyan runners.

In addition to being a journalism major, Phyllis had studied various languages in high school and college and had stayed up all night helping print the race information. As she handed out the brochures, she told the runners in their own language about the upcoming race.[4]

With less than two minutes to go, Sal opened the door to the barbershop and escorted Slim toward the front of the start. However, three men in dark suits and sunglasses knocked Sal down and grabbed Slim and took him to the extreme back of the pack which was on the finish line. At this time, Edna, who had been standing at the back of the pack, stood on top of a golf cart which was being run by an elderly gentleman with a patch over one of his eyes. She waved her arms to get the attention of the clown and pointed at Slim who was standing behind the other four thousand runners.

The clown ran a few steps to the side to get a better angle to see what was going on at the finish line. He saw three men in dark suits and sunglasses. They were shaking hands and moving away from the crowd. He could also see that the wheelchair entrants who were stationed at the back were all turning their wheelchairs to face the end of the race and that there were enough wheelchair people to be two deep all the way across the road. Slim then moved in front of the wheelchairs so that his right foot was almost touching the finish line. The wheelchair contestants were all patients at Edna's home and the clown could see the silver haired geriatric set waving at him.

With less than thirty seconds to go for the start of the race, the clown picked up the megaphone. He announced to the runners that because of the wind conditions it had been determined that the race would be run backwards and that everyone should turn around to begin the race. Amazingly enough, there was a minimum of confusion as the runners turned so that Slim was now toeing the new start line. Two rows of wheelchair contestants were immediately behind him with all of the slow runners and race walkers now at the front of the pack. The elite runners were over a block behind.

The clown raised the gun to start the race and at the stroke of 7:00 a.m. on the courthouse clock, the gun went off. So did Slim. But that was all. The wheelchairs were all in a locked position and did not move. A golf cart with the one-eyed man followed Slim on the road out of town, but there was grid-lock at the new starting line. The motorcyclists fell in behind Slim since no one else was involved in the running.

After about ninety seconds, some of the runners were able to get the wheelchairs started and slowly the runners and race walkers started plodding their way down the road. After approximately four minutes the elite runners who were now at the back of the pack had advanced almost halfway to the starting line. The clown who was the starter announced the prize money for the winners would be deferred until the Des Moines race. The runners, regardless of nationality and primary language, understood after Phyllis interpreted. They realized that their times were not going to be competitive and they decided that this should be a conditioning race for half the distance. Most elected to stay another week in Iowa and then competitively run the following week's race. Most of the elite runners had never run at a slow pace and they became anxious to find out for themselves what it would be like to spend over two hours jogging a half marathon.

Slim was past the three mile mark before the next group of runners reached the one mile mark and at that time no serious contender had gone more than three blocks to the edge of town. By this time Slug had turned the police car around and was sitting in park knowing that instead of leading the fastest runners he would now be pursuing the slowest runners. The reporters got off his car and went back to Des Moines realizing that this fiasco would not be newsworthy.

The three men in the dark suits and sunglasses headed for the pay phone which had been used to summon the ambulance for Roger and there they dialed a number in Las Vegas where the disastrous turn of events was relayed to their employer. As they were explaining the details of the current situation, the clown, who was escorting Sal, approached the men and asked to speak to their boss. He then assured the gaming executive that the marathon was indeed legal and would run the full course, only backwards. There was no rule against running the race in a different direction as long as the race officials (Sal's committee) had agreed to it which he assured the gambler that they had.

Both the gambler and the clown knew that if Slim won the race that the pay off would probably bust the casino which took the wager. The next few minutes were fraught with negotiations. It was finally agreed that all of the town's money would be returned along with a bonus of $1,000,000 in exchange for Sal voiding the bet. The million dollars would be given to the city for whatever purposes the mayor would deem advisable, such as spending part of it to purchase a restaurant business which would soon be sold. The building could be turned into a city owned tourist attraction since it was obvious that people would travel hundreds of miles to visit the home of the infamous soup.

The final stipulation was that Sal would receive three all expense paid trips to Las Vegas each year with the casino providing him with $3,000 in chips and tokens each time that he would make the trip.

After the deal was made and the phone call completed, the clown raced back to the finish line, which of course was now the starting line, and at that time the hot air balloon descended on the nearly deserted street. A second clown was manning the balloon with Eric and Phyllis also in the gondola. The first clown jumped in as the balloon started to ascend. As the four were ascending above the business district, Edna yelled at the clowns. She told them that she would see them at the revival area assuming that Rachel would stay on at the nursing home and take care of the few remaining patients who had been unable to help in the early morning activities.

They then watched Edna drive unobstructed along the original marathon route toward the revival grounds so she could help prepare for the oncoming crowd.

[4]. Phyllis later admitted she mistakenly told a Russian runner, "Pree vy'et! Pa'ssmoornah s-yehvo'dnya oo'tram. Par'ah za~ftrakat? Kako'y nash no'mer?" Which in English translates as:
"Hello, It's cloudy this morning. It's time for breakfast. Which is our room?" She knew as soon as she said the last sentence that she made a faux pas, especially when the runner smiled and pointed toward a window on the third floor of the rundown Sam Hill Hotel, near the library.

25

RACING TO THE REVIVAL

Slowly the balloon ascended over the town and softly started drifting toward the revival area. The air was still and hot and the cloud cover continued to cover the sky. As the identical clowns and Phyllis and Eric floated over Baker Street, they could see William and Eleanor and Cindy getting into the mayor's car enroute to the revival area. They continued to ascend and as they floated over the town limit, they could see a very tiny Slim Sims accompanied only by a golf cart and several dozen motorcyclists in single file procession. Much, much further behind was a group of wheelchairs going in a "V" formation similar to a flock of geese flying in their annual migration. Behind them was a solid wall of runners and walkers who, from this height, appeared to be pulled along by the flock of geese much like the pull of nature forces lemmings to the sea.

Far, far behind, still at the starting line, was the police car. An arm was sticking out of the driver's side of the car and pounding on the door in frustration over the unaccustomed lack of speed which the vehicle was forced to go.

Slowly and silently the balloon drifted over the plush farmland. Barry and Phyllis enjoyed the tranquil moments as they floated over the squares of cornfields, bean fields and pasture land. All the while Benny was concentrating on the messages that he would be soon delivering through the megaphone above the crowd near the famous covered bridge.

26

SLIM GOES HEAD OVER HEELS

As the balloon quietly drifted out of town, the airborne passengers glided over Edna's facility. Far below they could see Rachel and the remaining ambulators from the nursing home picking up the grounds and rolling up the canvas from the large tent. On the other side of the home they could see a rowboat anchored in the middle of the pond. In the boat were two old men huddled together and passing a flask.

Joe Dermotts had returned from his vacation late Friday night and had stopped at the judge's home to catch up on local gossip. He was stunned to find out that his rather upstart niece had helped to uncover the biggest story in Sam Hill since the cob fire many years before. He was so upset that the young woman had unearthed this story that he and Frank sat up all night finishing off several half full bottles of the judge's Southern Comfort. By early morning they had concluded that Dermotts should take retirement along with the judge so that they could enjoy each others company daily. They both realized that if Frank were to take to drinking alone he could be considered an alcoholic and it would therefore be best for both of them to drink together and retirement seemed the best avenue to accomplish this goal. Having thus made such a monumental decision, they agreed to spend the next day fishing in Edna's pond.

Several years earlier they had discovered that the pond had fish in the middle and every Saturday and Sunday morning before dawn they would go to the pond and fish for a few hours before the residents would wake up and see them. This was a great lasting secret that the judge and Dermotts had kept and they were very proud that no one else knew of this glorious fishing hole. Secrets were very hard to keep in small towns and both of the men had inwardly smiled for many years about their secret fishing hole.

Judge Peck and Dermotts watched a gigantic hot air balloon as it passed over head. Dermotts mumbled that they soon should be leaving the fishing hole and that perhaps they should follow the balloon to see where it was going. The judge belched loudly; noting the fact that their flask was empty, he suggested they return to his home and finish the remaining stock of whiskey. They pulled up the anchor just as the still air started moving enough to let them drift to the shore.

As the balloon approached the area for the revival, the hub of activity that had been so prevalent early in the morning in Sam Hill was now observable on the hill around the covered bridge. Most of the runners had finished and were cooling off with the sports drinks and fruit being furnished by Benny's congregation. Also, most of the motorcyclists were milling around and Slug's car could even be seen pulling onto the gravel road at the edge of the campsite.

As the balloon started to descend, a strange sight caught the attention of Phyllis and the clowns. Just on the other side of the area set off for the revival was Slim Sims and a gangly female runner. They were on the edge of the old Johnson farmland and the girl was standing with her hands over her mouth watching Slim hurdle row after row after row of soybeans.

About an hour before, Slim had cruised to the halfway point of the marathon where he was told by Edna that the race would officially end there because the elite runners had all agreed to save their competitive run for the next weekend in Des Moines. Also there was something about Sal's problems were now settled. Slim shrugged at the news and went to the revival area where he was presented with a wreath for winning the race and a medal signifying his victory. After cooling down a bit, he was greeted by the wheelchair brigade and the first set of joggers as they came in. Then a most strange thing happened.

The first woman to finish the race shook his hand and introduced herself as Shawna O'Brien, a foreign exchange student from Ireland.

Her sweaty grip for some reason made him get goose bumps. She was so thin as to appear anorexic. Tiny muscles from hours of road work prevailed throughout her body and as Slim stared at her he felt awakenings in his inner most being. Her dark bright red hair and freckled face and body made him dizzy. Quite suddenly and unexpectedly, Slim was smitten.

Slim ignored the other runners and bikers and civilians who were slapping him on the back and jostling with his wet hair and wreath. Shawna could feel the power as it ebbed and flowed from her toward him and she, too, felt suddenly weak and perplexed by this situation. Without thinking, they embraced, holding each other's sweat covered body. Desiring solitude, they left the crowd and slowly walked toward the green farmland a few hundred yards down the creek from the covered bridge.

They climbed the barbed wire boundary markings. While staring intently into each other's eyes Slim confessed to Shawna that he wanted her as no other man had wanted a woman and he felt that she should be the mother of his children. He went on to tell her that he wanted to buy a small plot of land outside of town and there they would have the largest watermelon patch in the history of mankind. Every day and every night they would eat the watermelons to the rind and he would feed her the white and black seeds from the watermelon with his fingers.

As she took this in she realized that she was uncontrollably falling in love with the man who had whipped the olympians in the race, the man who had the wreath of victory, the man who could train with her and push her to personal records beyond her greatest expectations, the man who did not appear Irish, but could spin more blarney than any Irish man she'd ever met. She too was hopelessly smitten.

Slim then proposed. Shawna accepted. The adrenaline flowed and Slim started a dance that soon turned to a race and within moments he was jumping the rows of soybean one after another after another. Shawna wondered if there were any established world records for soybean field hurdling. She gripped her mouth with her hands at this miracle of life and Slim took his wreath in one hand and his medal in the other and leaped happily into the air throwing his treasures high over his head.

27

SLUG EARNS HIS PAY

After completing the phone call, the three men in dark suits and sunglasses walked across the courthouse lawn. Behind them Sal was doing cartwheels. Slug had released his three prisoners the previous night with the understanding that they would immediately leave town. As he sat parked at the old starting line, he could see the three walking across the road. He got out of the car, pulled his hat over his clean cut hair-line, approached them and re-arrested them. They protested that he must be mistaken but he knew that he had the right culprits since no one had been in Sam Hill in such apparel before. He then put them in the back of the squad car and continued to follow the runners as they slowly trekked out of town toward the campgrounds.

By the time they reached the campground, Slug was reminded by the three men who seemed to know all their legal rights, (probably much better than even M.C. Ullestad would have) that since they had passed the town limits he no longer had jurisdiction over them. They then tried to convince him that they would not return to town if he released them at the campgrounds. Being a law man for so many years, he did understand their technical arguments about jurisdiction. Besides, he did not want to fill up the only cell in the jail again since it might be necessary to use it for some other criminal element lurking about, namely one of those motorcycle rogues. The three men were released by Slug at the gravel road turn-off into the revival area, and there they were offered a ride on a golf cart by an old man only identified as Schumacher who sported a patch over one of his eyes. The weight of the two men who had to stand on the back of the cart where the clubs would have been carried greatly affected

Schumacher's ability to spin the wheels and accelerate at the speed to which he was accustomed and which always impressed Slug. However, when the patched driver found out that the oddly dressed visitors were from Las Vegas, a conversation ensued which made Schumacher forget about his speed and daring tactics with the cart.

Schumacher had been to Las Vegas with Sal on several occasions many years past and they had always remarked how much gambling time was lost when people could not swiftly cross the street known as The Strip. Even worse, whenever tourists or gamblers took the cabs or buses up and down the strip there was such congestion that walking would have been more time effective. Schumacher told the men that they should convince their employer at the casino along with the other casino bosses to close the strip to vehicular traffic and to only allow golf carts which could be modified to be like his. They could then zip people quickly and safely from casino to casino, thus increasing the number of pulls generated on each of the millions of slots up and down the strip area.

The three men, who had previously been depressed about the attitude that their employer would have toward them for the way they botched their job in Sam Hill, now became more positive. They agreed this was a great idea and that they probably could regain the confidence of their employer with this solution to the grid lock problem that was gripping their city.

The old man with the eye patch and his three companions with dark glasses were quite excited now about the prospects of this idea becoming a reality and Schumacher told them to hold on. They all gripped the most accessible part of the cart and Schumacher turned a knob on the floor of the cart and immediately the gears shifted and the little cart went into overdrive and sped off for the nearest farmhouse where the proposal would be called in to the employer of the men in dark suits and sunglasses.

28

GATHER TOGETHER
BY THE RIVERBED

It was mid-morning by the time the balloon had drifted to the campsite. The sky was becoming darker and a low level rumble of thunder could be heard in the distance. Some of the runners were soaking their feet in the trickling remains of the creek bed below the Roseman bridge, but most of the runners and motorcyclists were stretched out on the hillside enjoying the morning and the food which was provided by Benny's congregate.

The mayor, Eleanor, and Cindy had arrived and they found a shaded location where they stretched out and were enjoying the first layer of sandwiches from their picnic basket. As they looked skyward, they could see the hot air balloon growing larger and larger as it approached. The beautiful rainbow above the huge cross was impressive to all below. It came so close that the crowd could easily see the passengers in the balloon. There were two clowns with identical facial make-up and suits. One of them was holding a megaphone in preparation of addressing the crowd. The other was adjusting the burners to give a final WHOOSH in order to position the balloon for the impending sermon. A young woman was busy focusing and shooting a small video camera and the older local residents recognized Eric Erickson who was smiling and waving at the crowd below.

The clown with the megaphone began preaching. He spoke of Paul's writings about running the good race. Phyllis translated for all the foreign runners. He preached, for the benefit of the motorcyclists, the Old Testament stories of faith and deliverance through tribulations of war. He told how the armies of Israel feared Goliath and how the faith of David enabled the youngster to slay the giant. The crowd was listening appreciatively, but it was evident that there was no great hunger for conversion among this group of sinners.

The wind started to pick up and the sky darkened ominously. The crew of the balloon started working very hard trying to adjust the burners and fuel regulator and they manipulated and maneuvered the vent ropes as the balloon started wavering in the wind.

Even the inattentive members of the crowd below now started watching the struggles that were taking place within the balloon. The preacher did not waver, however, and he continued onward with the message of eternal life through belief in the resurrection of the Savior who took the sins of the world to Calvary.

Suddenly, a voice was heard screaming from somewhere on the covered bridge.

"SAVE ME! GOD, PLEASE <u>SAAAVE ME!</u> THERE'S A FIRE AND I CAN'T GET OUT!"

Thousands of eyes turned toward the bridge and in horror everyone realized that a fire had somehow been ignited and the old wooden structure was in a state of combustion. Two hands reached through one of the holes in the middle of the bridge as smoke and flames erupted on both sides of the young man who was trapped.

There was no way anyone could get onto the bridge and it was obvious that they were all to witness a horrible and grizzly death by the flames which were already starting to leap into the air. No one spoke. There was utter silence except for the sounds of the crackling fire and a couple WHOOOSSES as the balloon heaved and jerked above the crowd.

The preacher with the megaphone then told the crowd about Nebuchadnezzar ordering Shadrach, Meshach and Abendnego into the flaming fires of his furnace and how their faith saved them. As he was recounting this biblical message from Daniel, the other clown was strapping what appeared to be a bungee cord to his ankles. Eric was working the propane tanks trying to keep the balloon stabilized and Phyllis was assisting the clown with his ropes.

Suddenly a large bolt of lightning struck very close to the campground and as the thunder roared through the area a huge wind pushed the balloon directly over the covered bridge. Just as suddenly, the wind calmed itself. The clown's feet were now secured to the rope and he stood on top of the gondola and stared at the flaming bridge directly below him. Phyllis grabbed and aimed her camera. The preaching clown pointed his megaphone toward the crowed, and in a deep baritone voice, started singing,

"AMAZING GRACE, HOW SWEET THE THE SOUND THAT SAVED A WRETCH LIKE ME....."

Through the smoke and fire the balloonists could see the young boy surrounded by flames. The hole in the roof of the covered bridge was about six feet wide. The clown on the gondola took a deep breath and dived.

The video footage which Phyllis then shot was what the networks would later claim to be the best footage of the century. Doing a swan dive, the clown went straight down through the roof of the bridge and as the bungee cord reached its full extension, he grabbed the outstretched arms of the young man and the snapping effect from the bungee cord pulled them back up through the hole in the top of the bridge. As they appeared coming up through the top of the bridge, the voices of the deacons, elders, laity, Dorcas Society members, runners, motorcyclists, residents of Edna's home, and most of the townspeople could be heard joining in the singing.

"I ONCE WAS LOST, BUT NOW I'M FOUND, FOR GRACE HAS SET ME FREE."

The cord released them down the second time just as the balloon had maneuvered past the bridge and Eric and Phyllis were then able to bring the balloon down far enough so that the crowd could then catch the young boy and unstrap the cord from the clown's feet. By the time the rescue was completed, many hundreds of voices of acknowledged sinful wretches were praising the majesty of their Creator who alone could save them from an eternity of fire.

As the balloon was touching down on the ground, the blackened sky opened up and water deluged the area.

The rain washed the soot from the face of the young man. Slug had worked his way down the bank to the location of the rescue and was startled to see that it was his grandson who had been saved. The boy had taken the old corn cob pipe which the mayor had given to Slug many years ago and was trying to smoke some chewing tobacco on the bridge when the cob got too hot and burned his hand. He dropped the pipe and almost immediately the fire had spread out of control.

As the rain started to let up, it was obvious that the boy needed some attention for his burns and the clown with the megaphone asked if there was anyone in the crowd with any medical training. Carolyn Johnson-Rogers had been sitting with the mayor and Eleanor and Cindy. They were several hundred feet from the boy but at this point in time she and Rachel were the only remaining medically trained people in town. She quickly started moving through the crowd to see what could be done for the boy.

The motorcyclists were unaware of the plight of the town since it would be without the services of Dr. Kellem or Roger Klinker. The cyclists, who were located over the entire grounds, looked to a point just a few feet from the smoldering bridge and every one of them pointed toward one of their own who was shaking his head and look-ing at his hands.

He had tight blue jeans and cowboy boots under the leather jacket which was oiled so that the raindrops would bounce away. He was one of the few clean shaven cyclists and his long and dark hair was rolled in a ponytail. He was standing next to his Harley and he reached over and took out a bag from the side pouch. He then care-fully put the black bag on the ground and opened it. He reached in and pulled out his stethescope and name badge. He pinned the badge on to the leather jacket. It said Dr. Goodman. He put the stethescope around his neck and picked up the medicine bag which contained first aid material for treatment in emergencies such as this.

As he waded across the rising creek, he saw a woman coming from the other side of the creek bed. She walked up to him and said, "Doctor, my name is Carolyn, and I am a nurse." He handed her the medicine bag and together they walked over to tend to Slug III.

The thunderstorm abated as quickly as it started and a double rainbow appeared over the Johnson farm. The creek was knee high and a special baptism was performed on hundreds of newly saved souls that noon hour, including Rex Smalley, who was so large he had to be rolled down the hill to the swollen creek.

After confering with one of the clowns, the mayor took the megaphone and announced that the city would be using surplus funds which were recently discovered to cover the cost of completely restoring the Roseman bridge which was not totally lost when the rains put out the fire.

Later that afternoon Edna called Phyllis to break the story that Dr. Goodman had been out to visit the nursing home and that he and Carolyn were seen walking hand in hand around the pond. After making the call to Phyllis, Edna told Rachel that she looked very tired and she really should go home and get some sleep.

The next day Dr. Goodman officially announced that a new medical practice was being established for the town and that his office would be located at the nursing home.

29

VISITORS

Two months later Eric was back at his job on the beach. He would visit with the tourists and after determining what kind of credit cards they had, he would explain to them that he represented a competing card company and he would then hand out applications. Whenever the applications were processed, a distributors fee would be sent to Eric. The beauty of his operation was that he represented four major credit cards and no matter which card the tourist would have, Eric could give them a brochure showing a better introductory deal with whichever card they did not possess.

As he was leaving Waikiki after spending several hours of hard work talking to the bikini clad prospects, he heard his name. There, crossing the street from the ABC Store were Cindy, Benny, Rachel and a man who looked much like the mayor had when they were teen-agers. After a moment's confusion, Eric realized that it was Barry. He had never realized that he hadn't actually seen Barry's face for many years even though they had spent several days together a few months earlier. The brothers and their wives were taking a long overdue vacation and wanted to surprise Eric. Later that night, Eric was shown an article which Phyllis had written for the New York Times. It was a quite lengthy article about a film made in Dealey Plaza during the assassination and how it had been lost to history because of a drunken judge. It was now obvious that they were free and no one would again be after any of them.

Barry and Eric and Cindy then told Rachel and Benny what had really happened when Kincaid came to town. When Kincaid got side tracked with Francesca, they had decided to give Kincaid a present for developing their film. While Rachel cared for Zack, they secretly followed Kincaid and Francesca and took a movie of the two lovers with Madeline's camera. This was to be a surprise memento for Kincaid and that was the film that was given to him to process when judge Peck made his appearance and destroyed the processing.

They never told Kincaid that he was developing a present rather than their film and since he was in a hurry to leave town, they kept the undeveloped film for many more years. Finally, on this very day, the film was taken to a young Japanese processor who had never heard of Dealey Plaza so that it would make no difference even if he did review the film that he processed.

Rachel passed out the popcorn which she had just popped and she snuggled up next to Barry. Barry kissed her forehead and said a silent prayer of thanks for this woman who had always been the love of his life and with whom he could now be with for the rest of his life. Benny turned down the lights and Eric turned on the projector. They then watched the film which Madeline had taken and which clearly showed the president's car passing in front of the two boys of high school age who were innocently waving at the president and his wife.

WHAT THE SAM HILL REDUX

30

SOMETHING'S FISHY

Herm Sherman was on a natural high. He arrived in Sam Hill before the early morning hours. He had gone to see the Saint and hadn't had as much fun since he was a kid. Now, as the world passed from darkness to the shadowy pink of pre-dawn that only early risers recognize, Herm walked down the path behind Edna's nursing home with two fishing poles and bait in hand.

The rowboat which was always available for traversing the pond was tied to the short dock. Herm climbed into the boat, released the rope from the dock and rowed to the middle of the pond where he remembered catching catfish several years ago when he was home on furlough.

He gently baited the treble hook and lowered it over the edge of the boat. He then took a small seine which he had used to capture minnows by the edge of the dock and gently he lifted one of the small creatures from a bucket and hooked it through its back so that it would survive to tempt a predator.

Herm did not notice a lone duck watching him as it floated several yards from the boat. Herm checked the first pole and finding that no nibbles had yet occurred, he glanced at the minnow, pulled it in close to him and gently kissed it and then spit on it for good luck. As he drew back the pole over his head to loft the minnow toward a spot in the water several yards from the boat, the duck ascended from the water and started to slowly circle the boat.

Herm released the line and the minnow went tumbling through the air. Just as the minnow was splashing down into the water the duck swooped and swallowed the minnow. Unfortunately for the duck, the hook, leader and part of the line also went down its gullet.

It is hard to determine which was the most surprised- the duck, the fisherman, or the minnow. In any event, the duck with all of its migratory instincts immediately started heading high and south. Although Herm was surprised, he was not about to lose his equipment and he immediately pulled back on the pole. The bird, as could be predicted, started quacking in great pain and with great volume. Herm did not want to break the line so he pushed the release button and gave the bird some slack. The bird then started circling the boat since it was obvious that flight away from the boat would result in great pain.

The man and beast fought each other for the better part of an hour, the fowl refusing to be reeled in and the man refusing to release the line. It was a classic match. A great standoff.

Many of the residents at Edna's home were early risers, as is usually the case with older people. Several saw the great struggle taking place on the pond and when it became apparent that the battle could potentially last all day, the resident who was to have the first use of the boat decided to ask for intervention from the police department so that the boat could be made available.

Within a few minutes of being summoned, Slug Marshall pulled up in the squad car and raced from the parking lot to the edge of the pond where he pulled out his bullhorn and screamed at Herm, "RELEASE THAT DUCK IMMEDIATELY AND RETURN TO SHORE OR YOU WILL BE ARRESTED FOR TRESPASSING AND HUNTING OUT OF SEASON."

By this time Herm was sweating profusely and was concentrating so hard on the magnificent struggle in which he was engaged that his mind was not in proper sync with his ears. There were noises which sounded like voices and he though it was the duck talking to him. Of course, Herm had heard voices on many occasions during his rehabilitation so he tried to disregard the noise and concentrate on reeling in the flying antagonist.

A few minutes after the duck had spoken to Herm, things became very confused. A hand appeared out of the pond holding a

Swiss army knife which lunged towards the pole which Herm was pulling and suddenly the line was cut and the pole went limp. Herm blinked twice through his sweat covered brow and watched the exhausted bird drop into the water several yards away. Herm shook his head hard to clear the sweat and when he again looked at the bird, he could see that the bird was staring back at him with crossed eyes. Herm turned and saw a policeman in full uniform holding onto the boat. Herm then realized that he must not have been quite to the drop off since the officer was only knee deep in the water. But what confused Herm most of all was that the officer was placing handcuffs on his wrists and asking questions about his clothing. As he looked down he could see that his tennis shoes, overalls and government issued blue shirt were all soaked with blood.

31

THE BIRD'S ON THE WING

In Sam Hill, as elsewhere, late May is the mating season for red-winged blackbirds. For a period of about five weeks each year, the overly excited males perform a ritual which is most disconcerting to anyone traversing the block which contains the courthouse.

On this particular morning, M.L. Ullestad was observing the frenetic birds from his second floor corner office in the courthouse. It was going to be a beautiful day, which meant that it would be slow for any business which would be required of him in his capacity as both county and city attorney. People would much rather be enjoying any type of outdoor activity than presenting him with issues of conflict which must naturally occur whenever communities form.

The courthouse had only been open twenty minutes and already three people who had intentions of entering had decided against it. The main reason, however, was not because of the wonderful weather, but was because of the blackbirds which were perched in the elm and willow trees surrounding the courthouse. Every time a person would invade the territory of the testosterone enhanced birds, the red-tipped wings would spread and the birds would dive at the unsuspecting human. Ullestad could not figure out if the birds were merely protecting their territory or if they thought that the hair on the heads resembled a nest. Regardless of the reason, the birds would swoop within inches of their targets and on occasion a claw would actually brush against the hair.

Ullestad turned from the window and sat down behind his desk. He had the desk since he began practicing forty years earlier. The mahogany top had been stained many times over the years and the credenza, which was added about twenty years later, did not match.

The old ceiling lights did not provide a great deal of illumination, but on days like this, the sunlight through the three large windows facing the street adequately illuminated the entire room. The sunshine caused the dust to sparkle on the set of Annotations and Northwest Reporters which filled one entire wall of the spacious room.

The two wooden chairs to be used by clients and bureaucrats on official business matched Ullestad's desk chair as all three were provided by the county and, which along with his desk and coat tree, comprised all of the furniture in the office. In the corner opposite the library materials was a file cabinet which had three drawers filled with files on cases involving prosecutions and records of council meetings, while the fourth drawer contained the files of Ullestad's private practice.

As the county attorney put his coffee cup on his desk and started to sit, he noticed that the door to his office was nearly closed. He then reached into the wastebasket to the right of his desk and picked out one of the several pieces of paper which had been rolled up like a basketball. An experienced flick of the wrist resulted in the paper flying over the top of the door and through the opened window separating the door from the ceiling, which is familiar to the architecture of older public buildings in the Midwest.

Ullestad's secretary, Ms. Henshaw, was officed in the tiny waiting area between Ullestad's office and the open spaces in the center of the courthouse. Her desk was situated so that the missiles which came from the inner office would land on her desk. As if by reflex, she took the stopwatch next to her typewriter and started it. However, when she saw that the door was half open, she stopped the watch and ventured toward Ullestad's office. She pushed her glasses further up to the bridge of her nose and asked the county attorney if the door was to be open or shut. He told her that he would not be working on any private cases until later so she pushed the door completely open.

The door squeaked as it opened. The door had made the same squeaky noise every time it had been opened and shut over the last twenty-four years. Ullestad could still remember a time when it did not squeak, but that was long before Ms. Henshaw obtained her employment only fifteen years ago. Several times over the years the thought had crossed Ullestad's mind that the squeaky door should be fixed before he retired, and once again this thought, or at least fragments of it, made a slight impression somewhere inside his head.

The understanding between Ullestad and the city and county officials was that the office and supplies were furnished because most of his practice was in his bureaucratic status and the door would always be open to the public during these times. However, when he had paying clients who had affairs to be taken care of outside the domain of the county or city attorney function, the door would be closed for private consultation and Ms. Henshaw would literally run the clock. At the end of each month, adjustments would be made for the time spent with private clients and Ullestad would then reimburse the governmental bodies for the use of their facilities.

With the door open and the sun shining through the windows, Ullestad pulled his chair next to the desk and put his feet up to savor the quietness of the moment. In the distance he could hear the police car's siren as it approached the courthouse from the west end of town. The sound got louder very quickly indicating that the driver was probably the town chief of police himself, Slug Marshall, who had a propensity to drive a little faster than necessary. Ullestad figured that Slug must be bringing in a new prisoner, which meant that he would be called upon shortly for an arraignment.

32

HERM

The new black and orange squad car halted on the west side of the courthouse. A deputy emerged from the passenger side and started running around the courthouse. The blackbirds lifted from their perches high in the trees, started to circle as they took aim on their prey, and swooped down toward the target which was scampering around the courthouse at a sprinter's speed.

Slug turned off the engine and opened the drivers' door. He then opened an oversized umbrella and stood next to the rear door, much like a chauffeur protecting his wealthy employer from the rain. Herm, handcuffed and staring vacantly into space, came out from the back seat and was led by Slug into the courthouse at a brisk pace. A thin young woman with long straggly blonde hair had been standing across the street chain smoking. She took advantage of the diversion caused by the deputy and followed Slug and Herm into the court-house.

Ullestad still had his feet on the desk when Slug brought Herm into the office. Ullestad, like most people in Sam Hill, had known Herm since he was a youngster. Herm had graduated from high school and gone directly into the Army. He had been captured by the North Vietnamese and was a prisoner of war for about four years. After being freed by virtue of a heroic mission involving at least one other Sam Hillian, Herm was returned to the States and there he went through long and painstaking rehabilitation. He was diagnosed as having the classic symptoms of post-traumatic stress disorder.

Over the years Herm would show improvement for periods of time but then would regress into states of mental and physical dysfunction. When in remission, he would be given furlough and each time he would quietly spend these calm periods in Sam Hill. As Ullestad studied Herm's vacated eyes and blank face, it was apparent that Herm had recently experienced some sort of trauma and Ullestad assumed the blood clotted clothing probably had something to do with it.

Slug briefed Ullestad on the confrontation at the pond so that Ullestad could make a determination on charges. Slug was quite certain that Herm had escaped from the VA hospital and had probably slipped into this catatonic state either before or after killing someone. It would be just a matter of time until a body would be found and until then, Herm would have to be held in custody to protect any other potential victims.

It was quite apparent that Herm certainly could not function by himself and custody made the most sense, even though Ullestad was not so certain that Herm could murder someone, since he had never shown aggression in his youth or while on his various furloughs.

Ullestad told Slug to take Herm to the jail in the basement of the courthouse. There they could get Herm some jail garb and take his clothes to the medical examiner for analysis of the blood. Also, Ullestad suggested that Herm be allowed to shower with the hope that if he got cleaned up and changed clothes perhaps he would come out of the trance and become communicative. Slug then led the bewildered prisoner out of the office and through the small waiting room where Ms. Henshaw and the pale thin blonde were seated.

The meeting involving Slug, Herm and Ullestad was official county business, so the door had been left partially opened and the conversations were naturally heard by the people in the adjacent room. It would not have made much difference even if the door had been closed because the window above the door was always left open.

33

ANOTHER NEW CASE

At first Ms. Henshaw thought that the girl was an accomplice of Herm. She was only a few strides behind Slug and Herm as they passed the secretary and entered Ullestad's office. Henshaw considered Herm a fright with all of the blood covering his clothing and his vacant eyeballs which appeared to want to pop out from his ashen face.

As the girl stopped directly in front of her, Henshaw had a few seconds to examine her. Beneath the dirty long hair was a face that probably could be quite pleasant with a smile and a modest amount of makeup. A blouse that badly needed an iron made it painfully obvious to Ms. Henshaw that the girl was not a believer in wearing a bra, and Ms. Henshaw immediately concluded that this type of girl probably had never even owned one. Several small tattoos of the home made variety were etched on the exposed arms and on the knuckles of the left hand. The long thin legs were scantily covered by a very short denim skirt and slightly above the cowboy boots, Henshaw notice a portion of another tattoo on the girls right leg.

Henshaw could not fathom why Slug would leave the girl unattended. Just as surely as Charlie Starkweather had Carole Fugate and Charles Manson had Squeaky Fromme, poor old Herm Sherman must have had this piece of white trash encouraging him into whatever awful deed that he perpetrated.

The young woman was in turn sizing up Henshaw. She determined that the middle-aged woman had been subjected to gravity for too many years and that the once fit frame was slowly being pushed downward and outward. Henshaw wore a business suit with a ruffled white blouse that buttoned just below the chin. The clean white fingernail polish displayed no dirt remaining under those nails while the young girl looked at her own dark red nails under which she knew was more than a bit of grime. The taller and younger woman, trying to avoid intimidation, threw back her shoulders causing her breasts to push forward, practically lunging at Henshaw, yet stopping abruptly and erect, much like a pair of hunting dogs on point.

The young woman opened her mouth and as she began to speak, Henshaw was somewhat surprised at the glistening whiteness and the perfect formation of the teeth.

"I need to see the county attorney about filing some charges to get my property back." The young woman said in a surprisingly husky voice.

Henshaw reached in her top right hand drawer and pulled out a questionnaire and pen and handed it to the younger woman. Henshaw nodded to the lone chair in the reception area and, without condescending to give a verbal reply, took the back of her hand and motioned for the young woman to sit and fill out the questionnaire. A few minutes later Slug and Herm came out of Ullestad's office and headed toward the basement. Henshaw took the questionnaire and took it into Ullestad's office. She then returned, and without speaking to or looking at the young woman, went back to her typewriter. A few minutes later Ullestad walked through the open door, looked around the reception area and after seeing the only unfamiliar face, said, "Ms. Peters, I presume. Please come in."

The young lady followed Ullestad into his office. Ms. Henshaw went to the door and started to close it since it appeared from the questionnaire that the legal matter would not be in Ullestad's official capacity. She then started the stop watch and went back to her work. Ullestad studied the questionnaire. The girl's name was Summersalt Peters. She was now residing in Des Moines but it appeared that a few weeks before she had been living in an apartment over on Baker Street. Apparently there had been a disagreement with her boyfriend and she left the apartment and he would not give her back some of her clothing.

Ullestad surmised that even though Henshaw's official evaluation that this would not be a criminal case was probably correct, he did not want to pay the city and county for giving advice on this case since he would not be handling it, anyway. So he picked up a piece of paper from the basket and flicked it through the window over the closed door. A few seconds later the handle turned and as the door squeaked half-way open, Henshaw's arm could be seen pushing from the other side. Ullestad waited until he could see Henshaw stop the stopwatch and then he proceeded to ask about the young lady's problem.

Ullestad could not help but think about Herm and the blood, but he feigned giving her his attention as she told him something about meeting an insurance man from Sam Hill while she was working in Des Moines and he then brought her to Sam Hill and rented an apartment for her. After several weeks there was a falling out and after having words, he summarily evicted her. She wanted him to return a sequined denim jacket and two pairs of snake-skin cowboy boots, which he had bought for her, but later refused to let her keep.

Ullestad suggested that the proper venue for handling this dispute would probably be small claims and that she could represent herself in this type of proceeding. Ullestad was not interested in spending a great deal of time on this matter and, without probing for any more details, started to dismiss the girl. However, she had a story to tell and she thought that the county attorney should at least hear the entire matter out before giving her this advice.

At this time the door made its squeaky noise as it was pushed fully open by Slug, who came barging into the office.

"M.L., I don't mean to interrupt but I think we have a serious problem with Herm downstairs." The chief was out of breath and had to take a few gasps of air before proceeding. Meanwhile, Ullestad, Henshaw and Peters all gathered around him to hear what he had to say.

Finally, he continued, "I took Herm down to the shower room in the basement and told one of my deputies to give him clean clothes and get him showered off. Herm went in the toilet stall and took off the bloody clothes and then came out and showered himself off good. The deputy then let him go back in the crapper stall to dry off and put on the prisoner's garb. Herm was in there a long time and the deputy just thought Herm was so scared that he probably was losing control of his bowels and bladder. Anyway, Herm stayed in there a long time and when Herm finally came out just a minute ago we discovered that he took his bloody clothes and tennis shoes and washed them completely clean in the toilet. Now we don't have a friggen bit of blood to give to the medical examiner."

Ullestad and Henshaw both stared at Slug with open mouths while the younger girl put her hand over her mouth to suppress a wide grin as she gently shook her head from side to side.

34

A THRILL FOR YOUNG SLUG

Summersalt went directly to the clerk's office where she was a line of one. After several minutes she was assisted in filling out the paperwork to initiate the action for the return of her property. Since she did not have the funds to cover the filing fee, the clerk helped her fill out the Affidavit of Pauper Forma.

After leaving the clerk's office, she went to the prisoner's hold in the basement and asked to see Mr. Sherman. She was told he could not have visitors until after being formally charged and then if he could not post bond, the visitation would probably be restricted to family members and counsel. Visitors in other categories could see the prisoners for ten minutes on Sunday between two and four o'clock p.m.

She then took paper towels from the ladies room and using these to cover her head, she scurried across the street to the corner restaurant. As she approached the entrance to the restaurant, she looked in the plate glass window which was acting as a mirror due to the position of the sun.

She could see one of the blackbirds crossing the street and diving toward her head dress. She moved very close to the window and as the bird lowered its beak and spread its clawed toes, she ducked her head and moved the towels against the glass. The bird was concentrating so hard on the towels that it could not prevent itself from smashing full force into the window. There was an enormous thud and the beginning of a cry from the bird, but because the momentum of the back portion of the bird pushed forward crushing the front, the sound of the bird was stilled. Momentarily, the bird was stuck to the glass just inches from Summersalts' eyes. Her first thought was that the bird looked like a mud ball that had been thrown against the glass. However, rather than oozing its way down the slick surface, the bird fell with a second thud.

Summersalt then entered the restaurant and found a seat near the window which contained a couple feathers and a little bit of slimy goo where the bird had impacted. A boy who appeared to be not quite high school age handed her a menu and a glass of water. She handed the menu back and said to the youngster, "Give me a cup of soup and glass of milk."

The boy looked at her and replied, "You must be a stranger to these parts, huh?"

She examined the youth, sat back in her chair and pulled her shoulders back. She could see the blood rush to the boy's face as his eyes widely opened. She tossed the hair out of her eyes and gave him a hard look. "Do you mean that I don't look familiar to you?"

The boy immediately started to stutter and stammer. Eventually he transmitted the information to her that the city council had passed an ordinance prohibiting the sale of soup within the city limits. At first she thought he was joking, but a quick examination of the menu verified that soups were not listed. She asked him whose great idea this was to exclude soups from the diet of the local population and the still flustered young man told her that it was probably presented to the city council by Mr. Ullestad and his grandfather, the chief of police.

Summersalt explained to the young man that her resources were limited and she could only afford soup and milk and then, with a big smile and again pulling her shoulders back, she asked if the boy had any suggestions. He immediately told her that since it was so early in the morning that he could give her a special on the blue plate luncheon and assured her that her funds would adequately cover the expenses. He then ran off to fix up her plate.

Several older gentlemen were having coffee a couple tables away from Summersalt, but because they were all nearly deaf, their voices carried throughout the dining area. They were already speculating about who the victim might be in the Sherman murder case. As the talk drifted to Herm's problems in Vietnam, Summersalt listened more intently, especially when they discussed Herm's memory losses and other quirks they observed when he had visited Sam Hill over the years.

Summersalt opened her purse and took out eight bottles of prescription drugs before finding the nearly empty pack of Camels and matches. She stuffed the pills back into her sequined purse when the young waiter brought out two large dishes of food. Then she asked him for an ashtray.

He backed up a couple steps and told her that she was in the non-smoking portion of the restaurant. She studied him with hard eye contact until the blushing again started. As she started tapping the cigarette on the table, she said to him in a very deep voice, "Non-smoking areas do not apply to people who are having nicotine fits."

She then flipped the cigarette into the air and caught it between her lips. Smiling, she handed the matches to the young man and waited until he lit her cigarette. He then stumbled twice before locating an ashtray in the smoking section and brought it back to her. Her smile became so large that he thought her lips went from ear to ear.

He wanted an excuse so that he could keep looking at her, so he said, "You know, I used to smoke, too. But one time I was smoking my dad's pipe on a bridge and set it on fire and this minister who dresses up like a clown or maybe it was his brother came jumping at me from a hot air balloon and he was attached to a bungee cord and he grabbed hold of me and pulled me from the bridge and dropped me in the water in the river below and ever since that time I haven't had another smoke and don't know if I ever will again."

Summersalt looked at him and asked, "Did you tell me you were related to the chief of police?"

The boy answered, "Yeah, he's my grandpa."

Summersalt crushed out the cigarette, and put the food in a napkin. She said to the boy, "Please don't have any children. The genes in your family are too regressive."

Summersalt observed the phone hanging near the entrance to the kitchen and stood up, saying, "Gotta use your phone a second, kid. That'll be okay, won't it?" As she reached the phone and started dialing, the young man started cleaning off the tables which were closer to her so that he could try to hear what she was saying. She was talking to a man because she called him Mack and she also told him that she needed to get back to work to make some bread. If he could find her some johns, she would make music with them. Slug's grandson had talked about this type of woman with his friends at school on many occasions, but he had never met one in real life. He could feel goosebumps all the way from his scalp down to his ankles.

Summersalt hung up the phone and started walking toward the door. As she started to pass the young man, she handed him a rumpled up dollar bill and a few pennies, told him thanks for the food, and gave him a quick hug. As she walked passed her table, she stopped and put down two cigarettes and a book of matches. Then as she opened the door, she turned to the youngest Slug and said, "Your tip's on the table."

35

THE CASE THAT WON'T GO AWAY

Slug was conferring with Ullestad. He had put out a search for missing persons in a six state area and he had already received back fourteen replies. Some of the missing people had been gone for several months and a few even several years. Although Slug was quite excited about the prospects at first, M.L. reminded him that if Herm had in fact killed someone, it would have been within the last day or two since the blood was still relatively fresh at the time he was caught and it had now been confirmed that he had only been released on furlough two days earlier. Slug still thought that every lead should be pursued and perhaps Herm had killed one of these people on a previous furlough and then boxed up the bloody clothes so that if he ever wanted to kill again he would not have to ruin more clothes. Even though M.L. agreed that Herm wasn't as bright as he was before his war experience, the suggestions of Slug were quite unreasonable.

Two FBI agents had arrived earlier in the afternoon and had requested to see Herm. Ullestad wondered why they would want to be involved in this situation. They reminded him that the federal government was responsible for the Veteran's Administration facilities and for Herm's rehabilitation and care. Therefore, there was a good possibility that if Herm had harmed or killed someone, there might be a civil claim for damages brought against Herm's providers, which would be the U.S. Government. The agents assured Ullestad that they would not be investigating any criminal activity but merely wanted to take statements to build a case in the event that any claim might be forthcoming. Even though the county attorney had informed agents Hosty and Shanklin that Herm would be non-responsive, they insisted on seeing him. It was then no surprise to Ullestad that the agents stopped back to tell him that they would need to wait until Herm became more responsive.

After the government agents had left, but while Ullestad and Slug were still discussing evidence in the case, Lester Lysol came barging in. Lester had graduated from law school less than ten years ago but had built up a formidable portfolio of clients because of his reputation for aggressiveness toward the adversary. He was the only attorney in the county who wore a suit to his office every day and today the well dressed lawyer appeared quite youthful as he interrupted the conversation of the older men who were very close to retirement age.

"M.L., what in the world are you doing representing that little piece of white trash from out of town against Grant Cooper?" the younger attorney asked.

M.L. quizzically looked at Lester and said, "Say again?"

Lester threw the small claims notice on Ullestad's desk and said, "My client is not only shocked that you would represent such a tart, but he has instructed me to counterclaim against your client for this public humiliation involved with this lawsuit and also for defamation of character and slander of his good name. And you may as well put your own insurance company on notice, M.L., because there is a good possibility that you may be sued for legal malpractice for filing such a frivolous piece of junk." Upon that, Lester did an about face and marched out of Ullestad's office.

M.L. picked up the paper and a frown went across his brow. Under the name of the plaintiff, Summersalt Peters, was written his name and office as her representative and attorney. He took a deep breath and reached into the wastebasket, picked up a waded piece of paper and threw it through the open door onto Ms. Henshaw's desk. She then peeked in the room and was told to get out the questionnaire filled by the young tattooed lady from earlier in the morning so that he could find her address and immediately let her know that she was not to use his name and that he was not representing her.

Ms. Henshaw brought the application in to Ullestad. M.L. told Slug to start looking for evidence on the Herm Sherman case and to re-check the grounds at Edna's for any clues that may have been left. After thus disposing of Slug, M.L. then took to concentrating on the immediate task of locating and dressing down Ms. Peters. However, when he examined the questionnaire, he discovered that her spelling was terrible and she probably was dyslectic. There was no telephone number given but there was a residence address in Des Moines. He told Ms. Henshaw to check the Des Moines City Directory for the location of Fifteen North Northeast Street. A few minutes later she reported that there was no such address in Des Moines. He examined the questionnaire more closely and saw that in fact the address portion really stated

Is No ne

Ullestad did not like this situation. He knew that Lester would be immediately filing a countersuit and until Ullestad could get in contact with the woman to get this straightened out, the court would expect him to act as her attorney. Suddenly, this insignificant matter became a personal top priority for M.L. and he sat down to think this out. He remembered looking out the window and seeing her either enter or exit the restaurant sometime after she had left that morning. Perhaps Slug III could shed some light on this. M.L. told Ms. Henshaw that he was leaving for the afternoon and he grabbed his coat and umbrella and headed for the restaurant.

Slug III was more than anxious to share with Ullestad the events of that morning, especially if it meant that the girl was in some kind of trouble and young Slug would be called as some sort of witness where he could again watch her as she threw back her shoulders and thrust those huge mountains toward him. After listening to fifteen minutes of rambling by young Slug, Ullestad determined that there was a possibility that he could locate this Summersalt. He picked up the phone and dialed the local operator.

"Lana, I am calling from the corner cafe and I want you to check and call me right back after you find out where all the calls went that were made from this phone today." M.L. then sat down and had a cup of coffee. A few minutes later the phone rang and M.L. picked it up. He took out a piece of scratch paper and pencil and wrote something down. He then said, "Thanks Lana, would you please call my wife and tell her that I need to run into Des Moines for a few hours tonight and I'll probably be home quite late."

36

MACK THE KNIFE'S

.L. had second thoughts as he pulled into the parking lot of the run down bar. It was a concrete structure with no windows and the neon arrow pointing toward the door was not fully operational. His car was the only standard vehicle in the lot. Motorcycles and dirty pickup trucks surrounded the muddy space that he found to park. Ullestad knew that he needed to talk to Summersalt as soon as possible, so he removed his suit coat and tie and entered the bar.

It was about what he had expected, except for the activities. On his left as he entered the door was a round card table. Two people dressed in cowboy paraphernalia were engaged in arm wrestling and behind what must have been the challenger were several people waiting in line to try to unseat the champion.

Luckily M.L. looked to his right before the next shot rang out. Near him at the beginning of a roped off area was another line. The young man with greasy hair and a rough looking beard was pointing a pistol at a target which was at the other end of the building in front of some sand bags. Just as M.L. was comprehending the gist of that activity, the pistol fired and Ullestad could see a tear in the heart of the target several yards away.

A small arena for mud wrestling was negotiated by Ullestad as he made his way toward the bar. No one was in the pit, but the mud had been recently watered and raked to allow a fresh activity for the patrons who would soon tire of the other activities.

Two snooker tables and a billiard table were on the far left corner of the building and a horseshoe shaped bar was in the middle. A stage with band equipment sitting on it was on the right side. M.L.

noticed that the only women in the bar were the waitresses who, as he expected, were scantily clad. Almost all of the patrons were extremely large men. M.L. had always considered himself and Slug the titans of the courthouse since they were both over six foot and about two hundred pounds each. However, he felt like a dwarf compared to most of these people. As he started to examine them more closely, he saw that they resembled the troops that he had occasionally seen on the professional wrestling television programs. About half wore the traditional cowboy outfits which are often seen in the truck stops along the interstates, and the other half resembled blue collar outdoors laborers who had not bothered to go home to clean up after work.

As Ullestad was making his way toward the front of the line at the bar, a burly hand tapped him on the shoulder. He turned and stared at a protruding adams apple from one of the widest necks he had ever seen. As he tilted his head backward and looked at the gigantic man's face, he could see facial scars and lines indicating a lifestyle much rougher than that for most middle aged men. The large man then said, "My office is across from the men's room behind the pool tables. If you are here looking for Summy, we can probably talk back there."

The large man's office was small, but it did contain a desk with a calculator and ashtray on it. The giant introduced himself as Mack and told M.L. that he was the owner of the place. After M.L. introduced himself and confirmed that he was indeed looking for Summersalt, Mack confided that since Summersalt had returned earlier in the evening, she told him that her lawyer might be looking for her and that he would probably be wearing wingtips and some dress clothes.

Mack took a bowie knife out of his top desk drawer and started cleaning his fingernails. M.L. had thought that Slug's Swiss army knife was large, but even in the immense hands of Mack, the steel blade was huge.

Mack said, "I want to get straight to the point with you, Mr.

Ullestad. The people who frequent my establishment follow my rules and my first rule is that nobody interferes in anyone else's business. The people in here and myself have pretty much taken care of Summy ever since she was a kid. She stays with a person here, and then for a while with a person there. She has no one to look after her except us.

"Summy was in a bad motorcycle accident when she was about fifteen and she was never able to finish school. She tends to forget things and sometimes acts a little weird. Most of us think it's because those doctors keep giving her all those pain pills. Sometimes she takes so many of them in a day that she'll get really depressed. We try to take care of her around here but sometimes she takes off and we don't see her for weeks at a time. I don't know exactly what she's been doing the last few weeks but I know from looking at her when she came back today that she has been on a real downer.

"Now I don't want to give you any advice, counselor, but if your business with her is causing any of this problem, I would think you would be best to forget about her and leave her be with those of us who care for her."

Then, to add emphasis to his statement, Mack fired the knife just to the left of M.L.'s ear and it stuck quite firmly into the dart board on the wall.

There was a considerable amount of silence as M.L. tried to decide what to do next. Suddenly, Mack stood up and said, "Enough of the pleasantries. Summy should be just about ready to do her thing. Let's go watch."

As the men came back to the public portion of the building, four members of the band were practicing. All of the patrons, without exception, were moving toward the stage area. Mack pushed his way through the crowd and hoisted himself onto the slightly elevated stage. He grabbed the microphone and after adjusting it to eliminate the screeching, said to the crowd, "Tonight we're proud to have the Johnnys here to provide the music and we're especially proud to welcome back our favorite entertainer, Summy Peters. The members of the Johnnys are Johnny Lenin at the drums, Johnny Marx on the steel guitar and Johnny Krushev on the bass. Finally, the last Johnny, Vladimar, `you can call me Johnny,' Johnson, will play the remaining assortment of instruments. Now let's have a big hand for Summy and the Johnnys."

The crowd cheered as the lights dimmed and a flood light shown on the side of the stage that had a covering which hid the performer from the audience. As the band did its prelude, the singer appeared and even though it was Summersalt Peters, M.L. had to blink his eyes several times because he could not believe what he was seeing.

As Summersalt came to the center of the stage, M.L. could see that her attire was not completely unfamiliar. She had on cowboy boots and a very short sequined dress with fringe coupled with a blouse covered with sequins that sparkled as the flood light changed colors. However, her hair was now washed and clean even though it still hung down and actually covered most of her face as she walked forward with her head partially bowed. As she grabbed the micro-phone M.L. could see that the red fingernail polish was replaced by a clear polish and that her long, neat and clean fingers were void of any tattoos. He did recognize the tattoo of the cat on her leg, but the rest of her body seemed remarkably clean compared to what he had seen earlier in the day. However, when she threw her head back and the hair flew from in front of her face as she opened her mouth on the first note, he was quite shocked to see a new tattoo of a huge black spider on her neck with a black web that spread out over the right half of her face. Also, black paint around her eyes emphasized the continuing dark mood of the singer.

The crowd immediately hushed as her mouth opened and M.L. was surprised at her ability to sing. The song was a Janice Joplin type melody and her low guttural sound impressed Ullestad to the point that he actually thought that this young woman could have competed with the previous generation's rock starlet. Summersalt not only sang like a professional, but her movements suggested that singing on the stage was her life. After the first song, the crowd cheered and stomped and put loose change and dollar bills into the can that Mack was passing around.

The next song was even more surprising to Ullestad. The band started playing a Whitney Houston tune and the deep husky voice that had so perfectly carried the first tune now changed in range and Summersalt switched to soprano effortlessly. Ullestad's mouth opened as he watched this strange girl perform. Again the crowd hooted and hollered in appreciation, even though they had been exposed to her talent many times before.

Finally, as the band started the final song of the set, all of the cowboy hats were removed in unison and as Summersalt turned and gracefully moved her hand toward the wall to the side of the band, everyone stood at attention and faced in that direction as a large American flag was unfurled. Summersalt then bellowed out a rendition of *God Bless America* that even Kate Smith would have been unable to equal. At the end of the song, there was absolute silence. Summersalt walked from the stage area back out of sight and most of the patrons unashamedly wiped their eyes or blew their noses with their bandanas. Ullestad could feel the body heat which had been generated by the emotions of the music and his face felt flush. He watched as the rugged men silently went back to the activities that they had previously left and within a few minutes, the noise level was starting to pick up to the accustomed level. Ullestad walked over to the bar where Mack was counting the money for Summy and the Johnnys and there he left his business card with a note for Summy to contact him as soon as possible.

37

SUMMY'S ON THE RUN

The mid-morning sun was beating down on the courthouse when a rusted out station wagon pulled into a parking spot near the corner cafe. Slug III was washing the large plate glass window when his heart gave a jump. He saw the back of the naughty lady as she was getting out of the dilapidated vehicle. His heart pounded even stronger when he saw her john, a giant of a man, get out of the drivers seat, open an umbrella and walk around to her side of the car. Slug was afraid that the john was here to work him over for letting her hug him, but the more he thought about, the more he realized that he had done nothing except give the naughty lady some food and maybe the john had brought her back to make her give him some more money for the food. As his mind raced from one fantasy to the other, he soon realized that the huge man and the lady of ill repute weren't coming to see him, but were hurrying under the umbrella across the street and going into the courthouse.

A few minutes later Ms. Henshaw opened the squeaky door and allowed Mack and Summersalt to enter M.L.'s office. Before M.L. could start any meaningful sort of dialogue regarding termination of representation on Summersalt's case, she told him that she wanted to see the prisoner. When Mack winked and nodded his head, Ullestad thought that perhaps there would be no harm in this gesture so he made the arrangements with the jailer and excused Summersalt, who looked different somehow even though Ullestad could not quite put his finger on it.

When Summersalt reached the basement, the jailer took her into a small private room where she waited until Herm was brought in. Herm's handcuffs were removed and the guard then left them in the

132

room alone while he closed the door and remained outside. It was the first time that Herm had neither been behind bars nor been handcuffed since fighting the duck in the boat. He sat at the table across from Summersalt and slowly looked around the room and also looked at his wrists. Summersalt reached out with her hands and with the tips of her fingers she lightly rubbed Herm's palms. He looked down at her hand and slowly the glazing left his eyes as he felt both freedom and warmth for the first time that he could remember.

Summersalt did not say anything, but continued to massage his hands. Several times Herm closed his eyes and slowly reopened them. Eventually he was able to look into the face of this person who was responsible for his new found freedom. His eyes locked on hers and there was a mutual feeling of seeing into the recesses of the other's head. She had the most beautiful eyes he had ever seen and he hoped that some day that his eyes could be as clear and pure as hers. He could not understand what was going on, but he felt great relief in her being there. Slowly he moved his eyes to examine her other features and he saw that she had a beautiful dove tattooed on each of her cheeks between the earlobe and the corner of her lips. As his eyes wandered he also saw in the creases of her forehead a red winged blackbird and on both sides of the bird were opened umbrellas pointing at the bird.

This was the most exciting and wonderful woman Herm had ever seen. He still didn't know where he was or why he was there, but for the first time he was happy with his plight. Slowly, Summersalt's blood red lips opened and he could see the tongue start to move between the beautifully aligned white teeth. Softly and slowly she told him not to worry. She also said that she was here to help him and that she knew what he was going through because she also had problems like he did. He knew that she was telling the truth and he trusted her immediately.

She asked him if he could remember what he was doing before he went fishing and try as he could, the only thing that he could remember was that he had gone to see the Saint and it had been like they were kids. However, he had not talked to anyone since his arrest and even though he wanted to tell her everything he knew, it was very difficult. She continued to massage his hands and slowly she went through the same question. Still Herm was unable to respond.

Summersalt was very patient. After many more minutes, she again talked to Herm and finally he was able to speak. He could say nothing more than what was necessary to answer her question because at this point it was very difficult to remember anything else and he was starting to get a headache. However, he wanted to tell her so much that he eventually managed to say that he went to see the Saint and it was fun like when they were kids. After saying this, his chest heaved and he closed his eyes.

Summersalt squeezed his hand and whispered to him that it would be all right. She told him to be courageous and that she would return to help him in any way possible. The jailer was then returning to the room and at that time he re-cuffed Herm and took him back to the cell where Herm would again become despondent and escape into catatonicism. Meanwhile, for the first time as far back as she could remember, Summersalt felt that she was needed and that she had a mission to accomplish. She went into the ladies room and took two bottles of her strongest medicines and threw them into the waste-basket.

Mack was giving Ullestad more details about Summersalt. He told M.L. how Summersalt's mother had worked in the mattress factory during the Vietnam war. Her husband who was the father of her other children was gone and she was a woman who could not suppress her desires. Consequently, she spent many afternoon testing the mattresses with various employees of the company and the father of Summersalt was one of possibly twenty or thirty men.

Summersalt's mother did not enjoy pregnancy and in her seventh month, she decided to terminate her pregnancy. She went to visit her aunt, who also was a midwife, and when the aunt went to fix tea, Summersalt's mother bended over, grasped her ankles, ducked her head, and went head over heels, again and again, until she felt the baby rebelling inside her. This induced her labor and within a few minutes Summersalt was born, although quite prematurely.

The mother already had several children to take care of so Summersalt was left with the midwife aunt. No birth certificate was obtained and no official name was ever rendered. After a couple years, the aunt decided to move to California and one night she took the baby to Mack's bar and later left without the baby. From that time on Mack and his customers raised the child, who, considering the circumstances, grew up to be quite normal until the motorcycle accident.

At this point in the conversation, Summersalt returned from downstairs and grabbed Mack.

"We gotta go, quick, cause I need to find something out." She exclaimed. Mack shrugged, told Ullestad that he would talk to him later and, grabbing the umbrella, followed Summersalt out of the room, closing the squeaky door behind him. Ullestad, scratching his balding head, was still trying to figure out how, and when, he would be able to get out of this case.

In the recesses of the basement jail, Herm stared at the back of his hands. Even though he could feel darkness enveloping his brain, he tried to focus on the wonderful young girl who had been so reassuring. He knew that if he could concentrate on her and the kindness she had shown, his soul would not become lost and he would cling to her promise that she could help him.

Upstairs, it was just the opposite for M.L. Out of sight, out of mind. Just as soon as Summersalt and Mack had left his office, two of the local boys who were attending the University of Iowa came in. They had made the Hawkeye football team and were getting ready to leave for Iowa City for summer practice. However, there was a great concern over the post season situation next winter.

Of the eighty-five major college football programs, only eighty teams would be able to go to a post season bowl game. The computers had projected that the Iowa football team would win only three games this fall. Under NCAA regulations, this would not be enough to qualify for a bowl game and Iowa had been to post season festivities dating back to when Hayden Fry had arrived on the scene from Texas.

Since most people were already making plans for Christmas, the bowl selection committees had already tendered their bids based on the projected fortune of the eligible teams. Iowa was not going to a bowl game this year! The women's field hockey and lacrosse team were scheduled to appear in Europe and Australia, respectively, for post season activities. The members of the football team felt that under Title IX, coupled with other federal discrimination statutes, a strong case could be made to force the NCAA to allow the Hawkeyes to participate at a major bowl game, even if it meant doing a double-header. M.L. had been researching out the statutes involved and sat down with the young men to analyze their rights.

Across the street, Slug III watched the naughty lady and her john race from the courthouse. The giant john reminded Slug of the bell-ringing hunch-back his literature teacher had discussed. The huge man was bent over holding an umbrella low enough to cover his head while also protecting the girl. The birds followed the pair as they raced across the street toward the office of the local newspaper, the Clarion. Slug III watched the couple duck into the old brick building and the birds, unable to find a clear target, returned to their roost to start a new vigil.

Summersalt and Mack were greeted by the oily smell of black ink and wood pulp as they walked toward the desk of the receptionist. Behind the receptionist was a life size photograph of a young woman not much older than Summersalt. Physically, except for the tattoos, they were very similar in appearance. Under the large photograph was the simple description

OUR EDITOR - PULITZER PRIZE WINNER

Summersalt asked if the receptionist knew anything about any local churches that had something to do with Saints and whether there were any old editions of the newspapers from about twenty-five years ago which would talk about the activities of the children of that time. The receptionist, who seemed to resemble Ms. Henshaw in both physical appearance and attitude, considered these rather unusual requests from the rather bizarre people. She wished to get rid of them as soon as possible, but without offending the huge man, so she suggested that they go to the library on the other side of the courthouse square for further assistance.

The early morning coffee clatche group of retired men had left the corner cafe and were taking up space at the barbershop next door to the cafe. They all gathered by the plate glass window at the front of the shop to watch a burly giant of a man with long black hair and a scraggly beard try to keep up with a young woman who came running across the street, past the cafe and barbershop and on down the block to the library. The next fifteen minutes was spent discussing who these people could possibly be and what they were doing running down the street.

After entering the library and taking a few minutes to catch their breath, Summersalt and Mack waited by the checkout desk for the return of the librarian, whose name plate indicated that she went by Cynthia. A few minutes later the silence was broken by footsteps of the only other person in the library who, by process of elimination, had to be Cynthia.

Cynthia, always sympathetic and attempting to be helpful as all librarians are, was initially befuddled by Summersalt's request for information. Although she knew nothing about any Saints at the churches, there was an archives in the basement of the library where old newspapers and yearbooks from the local high school were kept. Cynthia asked the excited young lady if there were any more specific pieces of information that could be shared and Summersalt then told her that she needed to find out about Herm Sherman as a child.

Cynthia said that her brother-in-law had once gone on a mission to rescue prisoners of war in Vietnam and it ended up that one of the rescued people was Herm. Summersalt immediately interrupted and wanted to know how to contact Cynthia's brother-in-law. Cynthia said that he was now working in Dallas and wrote down the address on an overdue fine receipt. Summersalt turned to Mack and said, "Mack, loan me some bus fair. Then call the Johnnys and tell them that when I get back from Texas I will do a couple jobs with them to get the money to pay you back."

Summersalt then ran out the library door and raced to Mack's old station wagon. Slug III again peered out the window of the cafe and saw the naughty lady standing by the old car. He then watched her john come up and take a roll out of his pocket and hand the girl a big wad of money.

"Holy crap," whispered Slug III to himself, "she's been doing tricks in the town library and now her john is giving her the money she earned."

38

ENTREPRENEURING IN BIG D

Summersalt waited for the bus on the main highway just beyond Edna's retirement home. As soon as she got on the bus, she had a premonition that this would be an extra long ride. It took several minutes for the bus to start moving again because it was time for a change of shift at the packing plant two blocks from Edna's and the employees were backing up traffic. As Summersalt found a seat and tried to get adjusted for the long ride ahead, she opened her purse to see if she had an adequate supply of pills to help her with the anticipated discomfort of the lengthy journey. She saw that she had a fairly good supply yet of Naprosyn, Cyclobenzaprine, a few Demerol, some Tylenol 3 and of course a few pills containing morphine and belladonna.

As the hours dragged on, she popped pill after pill to counteract the headaches and mid back pain, but it was a losing battle and she was unable to rest during the entire trip.

By the time the bus arrived at the renovated station near the west end of downtown Dallas, which was nearly a full day later, Summersalt was feeling herself go on a real downer. She went into the women's room in the bus station and looked in the mirror. The doves and blackbird and umbrellas were no longer appropriate so she took out the baby oil and vigorously washed her face until the tattoos were completely gone. The pills had been ineffective for her headache, and she was having trouble remembering exactly why she was in this strange place. She pulled out a few more pills and after swallowing them, she took out several tattoos which she placed on the wash basin and then looked at the image in the mirror to decide what her appearance should be.

After eating a small meal and obtaining directions to the address on the overdue book fine receipt, she left the bus station and walked west two blocks to Houston Street. There she caught a southbound bus which took her away from the downtown area and over the viaduct. She got off at Beckley and then walked about six blocks on Beckley Street toward Jefferson. When she saw the sign that said Neely Street, she turned right and sure enough it was only a block and a half to 214 Neely.

The Oak Cliff portion of Dallas was very run down, but Summersalt was not intimidated by the environment. There were two tour buses in front of the old two story house at 214 Neely. The yard was enclosed with a fence and the tourists from the bus were standing in line outside a gate which led around the house to the back yard. A young man was taking admission of $3.00 per person from the Japanese tourists.

Summersalt walked up to the money taker and said, "I am from Iowa and Cynthia, the librarian at Sam Hill, told me to talk to her brother-in-law who apparently has bought this house."

The young man said, "Barry is not here. He was called to handle an oil rig emergency down the road a piece."

Summersalt could not retain her composure anymore, and she started crying. She told the young man that she needed to see the owner right away and she was almost out of money.

The young man considered her dilemma for a minute, and then suggested, "I am sure that since you are from Mr. Sardinhurst's area that he would want me to take care of you. Why don't you go in the back yard and use the old Imperial Reflex Camera to take the pictures of the tourists. If you would do this for a couple hours, I can pay you enough money to catch a bus which will take you right by the fields where Barry is working."

Summersalt then went to the back yard. She saw a life size poster of a body of a man dressed in black. In his left hand he was holding a rifle and in his right hand were two newspapers. A pistol was strapped around his waist. The poster was from the neck down and the tourists could stand behind the poster and have a picture taken which would then show the head of the tourist on the body of the poster. Summersalt realized that this was a replica of one of the pictures taken of Lee Harvey Oswald by his wife which he contended was a fake.

The old house where Oswald and his wife had lived became run down over the years and Barry Sardinhurst had bought the house for back taxes a few months ago. He then reconstructed the back yard to be identical to the way it was in 1963 and the poster was then placed where Oswald allegedly stood when the infamous pictures were taken. Now, for a mere three dollars, any tourist could stand behind the impostor poster in the same back yard and have a picture taken with their head on Lee Harvey Oswald's body.

An auburn wig with short hair was given to Summersalt and she then spent the rest of the afternoon pretending to be the alleged assassin's wife taking pictures of tourists with a replica camera that was used many years ago.

In a remote village in Japan, many years from now, and perhaps even generations from now, the stories will continue to be told about how the ageless young wife of the president's assassin, who had a large tattoo of a werewolf covering half of her face, had taken pictures of the Yukomoto brothers while they toured America.

39

DOWN TIME

The bus dropped Summersalt off on a long, dusty, seemingly endless stretch of road miles from the nearest town. Several hundred yards away she could see a drilling rig pyramiding high off the flat horizon. There were several trucks and hard hat workers circling the large rig. Most of the men were looking intently at the rig through binoculars. Summersalt approached one of the men who had the word "foreman" stitched above his shirt pocket and she asked him where she could find Mr. Sardinhurst.

Without turning, he said to her, "He's busy right now. He's part way down the shaft working on a malfunction in the blow out preventer stack."

Summersalt glanced at the huge structure and asked when Mr. Sardinhurst might be on break so that she could talk to him. The foreman, while still holding the binoculars in the direction of the rig, turned his head and grinned at her. "I don't think you understand, lady. The blow-out preventer stack is designed to contain pressures of up to 15,000 pounds per square inch. These rigs are operated by a computer called an electronic drillers console which is within the driller's cabin. There was a breakdown on the electronical information necessary to operate the rig and Sardinhurst is one of only a few people in the world who has the mental and physical fortitude to work on this equipment. Assuming that he can make the necessary repair to make the system operational again, he should be out shortly. It's been nearly forty-eight hours since he started this project."

Summersalt frowned and the furrows in her forehead made the bald eagle which was tattooed there flap its wings. The foreman smiled even more and said, "You're cute when you frown, kid." He turned his eyes back into the binoculars.

Summersalt then asked, "You said that he would be out if he's successful. Does that mean it will take him more time if he is not successful?"

The foreman kept staring through the binoculars and merely said, "There is a reason that no one is within several hundred yards of the rig. Let's just say that if he is unsuccessful, hopefully no one else will be hurt."

Summersalt did not know what to do until the result of Mr. Sardinhurst's work was known, so she sat in the cab of the foreman's pickup truck and listened to gospel music on the foreman's cassettes. After listening to a few songs, Summersalt jumped when she heard noises from outside the vehicle. The workers were cheering as the solitary figure was walking toward them from the rig. She watched the middle-aged man as he approached. He wore cowboy boots and combat pants with a tool belt strapped around him in the midriff. He was completely naked above the waist and dirt and sweat covered his frame as he came close. Summersalt did not read books, but she remembered the pictures of Fabio from the covers of the romance novels. Although this man's hair was not long, she was sure that if Fabio kept in shape, he would look like this in about twenty years. After Sardinhurst explained to the foreman what had been done to fix the rig, the crew went back to work.

After Summersalt introduced herself, she grabbed a towel and some soap and water which was left for the workmen. She offered to help wash up this man whom she had traveled for several days to see. Barry shrugged his massive shoulders and sat on the edge of one of the trucks while she started bathing him. As she cleaned him, Summersalt told Barry the story of Herm and his incarceration in the Sam Hill jail.

Barry was very concerned. Even though Herm was a friend in school, Barry felt a special kinship toward Herm since the rescue near Pleiku. Barry told Summersalt that he was not sure what it meant about seeing the Saint or doing something when Herm was a child. However, it seemed only logical to Barry that the missing pieces to this puzzle must still be in Sam Hill.

Most of Barry's family was still in Sam Hill. His wife Rachel had been staying there while he set up the project in Dallas and worked various other side businesses, such as the rig fixing venture. Yes, it would probably be best that he accompany her back to Sam Hill and that they restart the investigation there. Then, together, Summersalt and Barry Sardinhurst jumped in his jeep and headed away from the dusty plains of Texas and toward the green farmland of Iowa.

40

CASE CLOSED

There had been good news for M.L. His threat of suit against the NCAA had caused a minor furor within its governing body. The controlling powers offered a compromise plan to Ullestad's clients. The NCAA agreed to contact the promoters of the Boise Bowl so that Iowa would be guaranteed a game if they could at least win their non-conference games against the University of Dubuque and Kirkwood Community College. The local players figured that if they could not win at least these two games during the season they probably didn't deserve to go to a bowl game anyway so they accepted the compromise offer and the case was settled.

An even better situation was developing on Summersalt's case. Lester had convinced Grant Cooper that it would be far too expensive to proceed all the way to trial and that the best alternative would be to give the jacket and boots to Summersalt in exchange for her signature on a seven page release. M.L. was quite certain that this was all she ever wanted in the first place and told Lester that he would need to review the proposed release papers first and he would then talk to Summersalt and if agreeable, that case would also be settled.

M.L. did not understand why such an extensive release was required by Grant and his attorney. He decided to examine the release paper quite carefully and was surprised to see that not only were the litigants dropping all claims against each other, but Summersalt was promising, in her release, to destroy and never disclose to anyone what was contained in certain home movies which she may have in her possession. M.L. began to wish that he had paid more attention to Summersalt when she tried to tell him about her case and he thought that perhaps Mr. Cooper might want to sweeten the pot to insure that whatever secrets were contained in his little home movies with Summersalt would remain outside the public domain.

Ullestad decided to find out just exactly how important this portion of the release was to Lester's client. He called Lester and told his adversary that there were certain parts of the release that would be unsatisfactory to his client. Both men then danced around the issue for a bit and finally Ullestad indicated that the portion of the release pertaining to home movies would not be executed unless Lester's client could sweeten the pot and throw in some cash. There was just enough silence on Lester's end of the phone for M.L. to realize that he had hit a home run and there could be some money coming. When Lester finally asked if M.L. had a figure in mind, the sage old advocate told Lester that Mr. Cooper would have to make an offer and that there would be no counteroffer. Either the offer would be very adequate or M.L.'s client would publicly display everything she had.

Less than twenty-four hours later, on the floor next to the filing cabinet lay the sequined jacket, snake skinned boots, a cashier's check payable to Summersalt in the amount of $15,000 and the release papers which Summersalt would need to execute before receiving her booty.

About the only thing that had not gone well over the last few days was the problem of what to do with Herm. There were still no bodies that had been found and no reports of missing persons for the period immediately before Herm was arrested. The FBI agents were becoming irritants as they continued to hang around the courthouse and drink coffee all day, every day. The representatives from the VA Hospital were in town and examined Herm in his cell. They reported to M.L. that they would not take him back in this condition. He was fine when he went on furlough and they would not accept him back in any other condition. Also, if he was involved in some foul play, other than being involved in inhumane treatment to wild animals, their attorney had told them to keep a distance from Herm. M.L. knew that he couldn't keep Herm in the jail forever, but on the other hand there was no place for Herm to go. Ullestad doubted if any bodies would ever surface and it certainly would not be fair to the city to be responsible for Herm's board and room for the rest of his life.

It seemed the only thing to do would be to set up a hearing on Herm's sanity and if M.L. could convince the judge that Herm was a harm to himself or to others, then the court would be obligated to institutionalize Herm at a state run mental health facility. M.L. then summoned Ms. Henshaw with one of his crumpled pieces of paper, and when she came into the room, he told her to do two things. First, she must start the paperwork to have Herm subjected to a mental health hearing within the next few days and secondly she must get a new supply of crumpled up papers for him to throw at her.

41

MUTUAL REMINISCENCES

Summersalt felt very comfortable with this strong, older man. He listened intently as she rambled. She told him that in many ways he reminded her of her best friend, Mack, who was kind of like a father and who, with his friends, had pretty much raised her until she was a teenager. Then there was a time when she couldn't remember much except everyone keeps telling her that she had this motorcycle accident and all she could remember is that she was a young teenager one day and it seemed like the next day she was already through her teens. In between was some times in and out of hospitals and therapy and doctors and psychiatrist and psychologists and physiologists and pain in her back and terrific headaches and pills and pills and pills. Finally, most of the last couple years were pretty clear and she remembered the good times singing at Mack's bar and feeling real good sometimes and sometimes feeling really bad and rotten, but always Mack was there to help if she wanted it.

Sometimes she felt like she wasn't contributing to life but then there was this guy named Grant Cooper who saw her singing one night when she was feeling really good and she was feeling so good that she didn't even have any tattoos except for the real one of the kitten on the inside of her leg. Anyway, this Cooper guy met her and promised that he could get her a real job and that he would get her an apartment on the edge of Sam Hill where he lived.

He rented her an apartment but never got her any jobs. He would come over nearly every day and she would cook for him and give him massages and make him feel good because he was nice to her. But when she started getting her headaches again and needed to take lots of pills, he would get mad at her and finally he kicked her out and took away everything, including her jacket and boots which he had given to her as a present and had promised that she could keep forever.

Ever since Cooper got mad at her, she realized that most normal people would probably never understand her. But Herm had a head problem, too, and that's why she felt an instant rapport with him when she first saw him, and that motivated her to strike out on her mission to set him free.

Summersalt was quite exhausted after telling all these things to Barry. However, she wanted, even needed, to know more about Herm in the hope that she could better understand him and maybe even help him. She asked Barry to tell her all about Herm's confinement in Vietnam and how they rescued him. However, just as Barry started to tell her what he remembered, she curled her body up and put her head against his shoulder. He looked over and saw that she was fast asleep.

Barry turned down the radio and thought about Summersalt's activities over the past few days. Ever since Herm had managed to communicate his bewildered thoughts to her, she had been running around like a chicken with her head cut off. She had been to the newspaper and the library and then on the bus to Dallas and eventually to the oil fields where she had caught up with him. Then his thoughts drifted away from Summersalt and went back to a period in his life when he engaged in the rescue mission for the prisoners of war.

It had been over fifteen years since he and the other commandos had jumped from the huey into the sultry area west of Pleiku which was nearly on the Cambodian border. The years had dimmed the memory, but the hot Oklahoma air rushing through the jeep helped his mind dredge up the memories.

Barry had left his wife and family, but not for the same reason that many of the young men of that era were fleeing to Canada. In fact, Barry stayed within the United States for quite a bit of the time that he was in hiding. His best friend, Eric Erickson, had been drafted and sent to Vietnam. Several other young men from Sam Hill were also doing tours there when he learned that a wealthy super-patriot in Texas was hiring mercenaries to go into Laos and Cambodia to rescue prisoners of war.

The American Army would not violate the Geneva Rules and there were orders against crossing into those countries in search of hostages or the enemy. Barry, using a pseudonym and false identification, was hired by the patriotic Texan and after a few weeks of vigorous training in commando life, was transported with a half dozen other mercenaries to Kuala Lampore. For the next few weeks there was intensive jungle training and Barry and his compadres were given intense training in languages and the cultural behavior of the North Vietnamese soldiers. Finally, word came down that they would be soon moving into a position to rescue as many as thirty Americans who had been taken as prisoners and relocated outside the confines of South Vietnam.

Barry always figured that his employer at least had the tacit approval of the CIA, because the last legs of his journey after reaching Saigon were by military transport and no one checked the credentials of his party. Since he had no dog tags or other forms of identification, he assumed that he could have been stopped at any point by the military but instead it was as though he were invisible.

Barry remembered having to machete his way through heavy foliage for nearly three days before his squad rendezvoused within a few clicks of the main prisoner camp. After another twenty-four hours of surveillance, it was determined that they would be able to have the best chance of rescuing the prisoners without many fatalities by blowing up the three main guard posts and charging the encampment all in one motion.

About two hours before dawn the next morning the plan was ready. Three rocket launchers blew up the sentry posts, killing all the sentries who were on duty. Barry and four others charged through the gate and took out the remaining guards with hand grenades and M-16 fire power. The prisoners' huts were not locked and to Barry's amazement, there were over fifty prisoners instead of the anticipated thirty. The surprise attack had resulted in the remaining enemy immediately surrendering rather than face the alternative of likely death. By daybreak, the remaining NVA were tied, gagged and locked inside the prisoner's hooches. The prisoners were fed and most were able to walk. The slow process of getting back to the Vietnamese border was hindered even more because several of the prisoners had infections and a few even had gangrene. It took nearly a week to get them back to the pre-arranged point where unmarked helicopters processed them back to the hospitals near Saigon.

Barry had not known until the third day after leaving the encampment that Herm Sherman was one of the prisoners who had been rescued. Herm had helped carry one of the sicker prisoners, but Herm had been non-responsive to questioning and it was only after seeing Herm's dog tag that Barry realized that the gauntly man with vacant eyes was the war torn version of the carefree and happy youth that Barry had vaguely remembered from Sam Hill. The shock that ignited through Barry's body when he realized what had happened to Herm over the intervening years was probably greater than any trauma that he had endured to that point in his life other than the loss of his son. Barry had not seen Herm again after putting him on the rescue helicopter, but over the years he had followed Herm's progress and lack thereof through communication from Rachel. Barry never could figure out if Herm's condition may have been induced by trauma or by the general condition of living in the prisoner of war camp. This was one of God's little mysteries that would probably never be revealed. The only thing he was sure of was that Herm's unnatural condition was quite evident during the trek from the prison camp.

Barry leaned back in the driver's seat and looked at the beauty of the Ozarks of Southern Missouri as they traveled homeward. He reached over and dabbed the drool from the chin of the girl who was sleeping deeply with her mouth open. He felt a pang of sorrow erupt from his heart which ran completely across his chest. The sorrow went out for both Herm and Summersalt. They were both victims of cruel fate which arbitrarily captures some while ignoring others. Barry hoped that he could help with Herm's problem. By doing so, he knew that Summersalt would also be happy.

42

DETECTIVE WORK

Barry and Summersalt arrived in Sam Hill just as the shift change was taking place at the packing plant. The delay caused evident distress to Summersalt. Barry drove straight to the courthouse and suggested that she visit with Herm to see if any further communication could be made. He would then meet her later after having a chance to see Rachel, who was working at Edna's Nursing Home. Summersalt found an old newspaper in the back seat of the jeep and holding this over her head, she ran into the courthouse while the red-winged blackbirds kept watch over her. Ullestad had given standing orders that Summersalt could visit with Herm whenever she desired and she was allowed immediate visitation. However, it was quite evident that Herm had slipped back into the complete catatonic state and it took her a great deal of time to caress his hand to the point where he could respond to her.

Barry drove directly to Edna's Nursing Home. Edna saw him coming and invited him into her office for coffee. She told him that Rachel had taken some of the patients shopping to the Mega-Mall but they should be back later that evening or the next day.

Barry told Edna that he was back because of the business with Herm. Edna did not waste any time on small talk. She told Barry that a few days earlier Herm had come out of his trance long enough to tell the blonde girl from Des Moines that he had gone to see the Saint and it was like when they were kids. The blonde had disclosed this information to both the receptionist at the newspaper and to Cynthia, Barry's sister-in-law. Within the next twenty-four hours everyone, except possibly the workers at the courthouse, was aware of Herm's revelations and of course it would be a great honor to be labeled as the detective who figured out what this meant. Edna had taken it up with the ladies at the Dorcas Society and they had spent most of one morning discussing this. They had concluded that the Saint was quite probably John St. Gerald, a classmate of Herm's.

Barry was quite excited by this news and asked if anyone had talked to St. Gerald. Edna informed him that unfortunately John had died the previous year and had no family. Barry paced the office and stared out the big window at the pond where a few of the residents had caught some catfish from the dock.

After a few moments silence, Barry asked whether or not any leads were forthcoming as to the second part of Herm's remarks. Edna shook her head and said that was the part that had everybody stymied. Barry continued to pace and after several more minutes of thoughtful reflection, said, "If you are pretty sure that the Saint was John St. Gerald, then it seems probable that the other part relates to something that Herm and John did when they were children."

Edna nodded her head in agreement.

"Does anyone about our age remember anything that Herm and John did by themselves that would have been fun and yet led to the loss of blood? Did they have any secret societies where they were blood brothers, or anything like that?" Barry wondered aloud.

Edna shook her head. "We spent a great deal of time and effort just trying to answer the same questions, Barry. The few people who are still around that remember them as children can't recall anything at all unusual."

Barry stared out the window at the fishermen again. "Tell me, Edna, do you think Herm knows that John St. Gerald has died?"

Edna frowned and after a few seconds replied, "Now that you mention it, Barry, I doubt it seriously. John died within the last year and it has been over two years since Herm was last home on furlough."

Barry turned to Edna and said, "Where was John working the last time Herm was in town?"

Edna cocked her head and said, "Why, I believe that he was

working at the packing plant."

Before Edna could draw her breath to say anything else, Barry had turned and was out the door with a quick wave of the hand toward her. He then went back to the town square where Summersalt was waiting across the street from the courthouse. After she jumped into the jeep, he headed back toward the edge of town. As they drove past Edna's , Summersalt pointed toward the pond and turned to Barry and exclaimed, "Look, there's a duck near the pond with dental floss hanging from its beak!"

43

THE TRIAL

Even though judge Peck had officially retired, his pension was inadequate to maintain the lifestyle to which he had become accustomed. He therefore exercised his option to handle a few select cases each year. He insured that they were non-jury cases and were basically no brainers. When told that it would be a mental health hearing for a prisoner who was catatonic, Peck figured that he should volunteer to take the case.

As Peck looked down from the bench, he could see that the room was rather lopsided. On one side of the counsel table sat M.L. with Ms. Henshaw sitting next to him, ready to hand him the exhibits as they would be needed. To her right and just beyond the counsel table sat agents Hosty and Shanklin of the FBI along with a representative from the Veterans Administration. They were there to assist the court in finding that Herm had a mental illness which was of such long duration that it would absolve them of any responsibility for actions that he may have taken since being in Sam Hill.

Peck rolled his eyes to the other side of the table where Herm was sitting alone. The judge pointed at Ullestad and then curled his finger. Ullestad approached the bench.

"Don't you think that that Mr. Sherman should have an attorney?" queried his Honor.

Ullestad shrugged, and said, "Judge, he can not communicate, so it probably wouldn't do any good to appoint anyone."

The judge scratched his two day growth of beard and said, "Aha."

Lester Lysol had just entered the courtroom with several motions and orders for the judge to sign. But before the court would

156

consider Lester's matters, Lester found himself seated next to Herm listening to his name being read into the record as counsel for the alleged mental defective.

After a few opening remarks by Ullestad with a waiver of the same by Lester, the court requested evidence. Ullestad produced medical records provided by the Veterans Administration and was in the process of calling Ms. Henshaw to the stand to testify as to her observations of Herm, when the courtroom door opened.

Barry and Summersalt walked to the front of the gallery portion of the courtroom where they attracted Herm's attention. Herm, who was no longer handcuffed and was obviously not behind bars for the time being, was partially conscious of his whereabouts. When he saw Summersalt, he smiled and waved at her.

Barry then stood up and addressed the court, "Your Honor, with due respect, and without meaning to interrupt these proceedings, we do believe that we can provide an explanation to the court as to how Mr. Sherman came to be covered in blood which resulted in his arrest at Edna's pond."

The judge started to sense that this case could be getting complicated, and was not quite sure how to handle this. So he sat back in his chair and closed his eyes, pretending to be asleep.

After a few minutes of silence, Summersalt motioned toward Herm who got up from his chair and walked over to her. She then handed him a large sack and told him it was a present from the Saint and that he should have fun just like when they were kids.

Herm's eyes immediately lit up as he looked in the sack. Everyone in the courtroom except judge Peck then watched the sack fall to the floor as Herm held its contents, a pure white chicken. The animal had its head tucked under its wing and was sound asleep.

Herm moved to the small space between Ullestad, Henshaw and the government personnel. He then took the chicken's head from under the wing and tightened his fingers around the tiny beak. Then he hoisted the chicken into the air and let out a big warhoop.

Suddenly the chicken was going around and around over Herm's head like the blade of a helicopter warming up. Herm's right arm made larger and larger circles until suddenly everyone in the court-room, including judge Peck, heard a snap and saw the body of the chicken take off in the direction of the judge's head.

Just as Peck opened his eyes, he could see the headless chicken flying toward him with blood spurting out of the neck bone which was no longer connected to the head bone. The bird twitched and flew around the courtroom while Herm broke into loud guffaws. As the bird began its final twitching, it dove toward the people who surrounded Herm and its blood covered them like a spray from a paint brush flicked onto a canvas. The only one to escape the rain-like pellets of chicken blood was Lester, who immediately crawled under the table to protect his expensive suit.

After the chicken terminated its death dance, the judge looked down through his red spotted eyeglasses and saw Herm and Summersalt hugging and laughing while the others in the room were getting out their handkerchiefs to start cleaning themselves up.

Summersalt had called Mack who entered the courtroom and told judge Peck that he would act as guardian for Herm, who was making a remarkable recovery. The judge ordered Herm to be released and Summersalt waited downstairs while Herm was being processed out of the jail.

The FBI agents and Veterans Administration man grabbed their umbrellas and departed from the courthouse. Judge Peck went back into his chambers to have a drink and Ullestad, followed by Barry, pushed open his squeaky door and plopped down in the chair behind his desk. He looked at Barry and asked, "So how did you figure that out?"

Barry felt a little embarrassment since he knew that he would be considered the great successful sleuth of Sam Hill for some time. "It actually started when I saw some of Edna's folks with catfish on the dock. Everyone knows that blood is the best bait for catfish so I figured that Herm had probably needed some blood for bait to go fishing. Then when Edna told me that the Saint had worked at the packing plant, it became pretty obvious. Herm had not known that the Saint had died so he decided to stop at the packing plant to see Saint and pick up some catfish bait on the way to Edna's pond. He must have arrived during a break for the employees or even between shifts on the graveyard end of it, and seeing no one in the kill room, he probably just picked up one of the chickens that was ready to be slaughtered and decided to have a little fun. Last night Summersalt and I went out to make sure that the scenario was probable, and sure enough not only did we hit a time when no one was in the slaughter room, but we even took a free chicken out to be used as demonstrative evidence at your hearing today."

44

ALL'S WELL THAT ENDS

Summersalt and Herm walked into the office holding hands. Summersalt had told Herm about the Johnnies and since Herm's friend was John St. Gerald, they both believed this bond of common names was a sign that they belonged together. Mack came lumbering in just behind them.

After she signed the release, M.L. presented Summersalt with the sequined jacket, snake skinned boots and the check. Summersalt wanted M.L. to keep the check as his fee, but he assured her that this was a case that was done pro-bono and there was nothing due to him. Summersalt then offered the check to Barry for helping her get Herm released, but Barry assured her that with all of his ventures, he already had too much money. Mack declined the money because as the guardian for Herm, he did not want to have unaccounted for income where the government would require that the money be paid as reimbursement for Herm's costs over the years. Summersalt then decided that she could probably find someplace to put the money to good use, so she stuck it in the back pocket of her cutoff jeans.

It was then that M.L. realized that Summersalt was not sporting any tattoos other than the real one on her leg. As Summersalt tucked the check into her pocket, M.L. said, "That reminds me, Summersalt, there is a provision in the papers you signed that you must destroy any pictures or home movies that you have. As a matter of fact, it may be better if you just give them to me to insure that we are complying with the terms of the release."

Summersalt looked at Ullestad quizzically, and said, "Cooper was kind of funny. He did ask me to take some pictures of him, but I always just held the camera up in front of my face and closed my eyes cause he was probably doing something stupid and I really didn't want to watch. Most times I never put any film in the camera and the only time I remember having film, I did not turn the camera on."

Ullestad looked very disappointed. Barry immediately thought that Ullestad probably wanted to peruse the pictures himself, out of intellectual curiosity, of course. Barry then had an idea.

As the others were leaving the office, Barry hesitated and drew M.L. aside. He said, "M.L., Summersalt was too embarrassed to tell you the truth in front of her friends. She did have one movie changed from super eight to video tape."

Barry then reached into the thigh pocket of his combat pants and pulled out a video tape. He then followed Mack, Herm and Summersalt out of the room and he closed the squeaking door behind.

M.L. held the video tape in his hand and walked to the window in his office. He watched the four people huddle under an umbrella as they scampered across the courthouse lawn toward the corner cafe. As they reached the street, he saw them stop. Summersalt shrugged her shoulders and then took the sequined jacket and snake skinned boots and placed them in the Salvation Army bin. She and Herm gave each other a big hug and Summersalt then closed the umbrella and placed it against the bin. Summersalt and her three companions then crossed the street and entered the corner cafe.

Ullestad could wait no longer. He took the tape and slipped it into the VCR which was furnished by the county. He turned on the television and anxiously awaited to see what was on the film. Much to his surprise and bewilderment was the scene of a presidential motorcade from many years earlier traveling through Dealy Plaza.

Slug III dutifully served coffee to the naughty lady, her john and two other strangers who looked vaguely familiar. After they had conversed a few minutes and drunk their coffee, young Slug saw the man in combat pants pull something from his thigh pocket and place it on the table. A few minutes later the party walked out the front door. However, the naughty lady turned around and yelled to Slug, "You're probably going to need to go to college if you want to do something about your bad genes. Don't forget the tip, it's on the table." Slug went over to the table and looked. There was a book of matches, a corn cob pipe and a check for $15,000.00 which was endorsed to him.

The courthouse was closed and M.L. was the only person left. After looking at the video several times, and still being completely bewildered, he walked back to the window. He saw Barry jump in his jeep and head toward Edna's. Mack, Herm and Summersalt got in the old station wagon and also headed out of town. He then looked around the room and realized that his umbrella was gone. He again looked out the window and stared at the Salvation Army bin. There, resting against the bin was his umbrella. Perched on top of it with its wings spread was an angry looking red-winged blackbird.

IT'S A SMALL, SMALL WORLD

45

FLYING HIGH

Rex Smalley, because of his gargantuan size, had never been able to sleep on an airplane. An added problem to prevent rest on this trip was that he was concentrating very hard on a plan to make his death appear as a suicide. As he stared out his window in the first class seat, he managed a crooked smile knowing that he was leaving both Roseanne and the sprinter climate behind. It was that period of cold, slushy, cloudy days that was wedged between winter and spring which he called sprinter.

He knew that a direct flight from Chicago to Honolulu was much too long in the air but he would not have to deplane and he was at least in a first class seat. He had purchased a coach ticket but adjustments were made for boarding when it was apparent that Rex was too wide to navigate the aisle to his assigned seat. Even if the stewards had been able to lift him into his seating area, he would have needed two and one-third seats to control his massiveness. His mood was so dark that even the upgrade didn't abate his preoccupation with his plans for his impending demise.

Even in first class he needed both seats so no one shared his side of the aisle, which was just as well with him. While the plane still throttled over the mainland, though he was absorbed in his dark thoughts, he could feel the swelling of his feet and ankles. He had not worn laced shoes for a number of years because he could not reach around or over his inflated midriff to get to tie or untie the laces. Normally, he could slip in and out of his slippers, moccasins or loafers, whichever he was wearing at the moment, without difficulty; but today in the air the swelling already was such that he couldn't get his loafers off. Whatever remaining pride that he had was preventing him from requesting help, especially from Charity, in removing the shoes, so he grimaced and groaned as the stitching on the black leather shoes stretched and stretched and stretched.

The first class stewardess, whose name tag identified her as Charity, offered several magazines and books for Rex prior to take-off. His eyes moved much more quickly than his rotund body and his still lean and quick mind immediately realized that the young blond with a ballerinas' figure was indeed first class. Rex picked up one of the magazines in an effort to disassociate himself from his dark plans and aching feet, but the magazine was filled with articles on health, diet and longevity, none of which interested Rex.

Setting the magazine aside, he thought of when his body had not been so excessive. Actually, until his marriage at age twenty-three to Roseanne, he was quite fit. He was unaware that the food she prepared, coupled with the misery of the mismatched marriage to her, caused a problem until one day, after an exam by his family physician, Dr. Kellem, he peeked at his chart while the doctor went to the next examining room to counsel a pregnant girl, and Rex was shocked to discover that medically he was diagnosed as grossly obese. Later that day he looked in the mirror and saw what had escaped him daily as he shaved and reviewed his combed locks - he was indeed grossly obese. This discovery had been fifteen years ago but could have been fifteen hundred years ago, because ever since both Roseanne and his mirror confirmed his faults daily. He was especially aware of the ever widening torso and a receding hairline and the ever so slowly but gradually, never stopping, thinning of his once beautiful head of coal black hair which by now required only an occasional pull of a broken four toothed combed to keep the few remaining strands on top of the expansive head.

He closed his eyes in an effort to breath clean, fresh thoughts through the blackness which filled his head. Slowly, his mind forced away the image of his grotesque features and even more slowly the image of Roseanne, with her thick pointer finger in his face and her scowl and foul language and hot garlic breath blowing into his nostrils. The images drifted out of his head, left his body and floated out his window forming a thunder cloud on the port side of the speeding plane.

Rex tried to recall his childhood, the only good time of his life, as he squeezed his eyelids shut. He grew up outside Sam Hill and was a hero amongst his classmates. His fathers' cousin was the Roy Smalley, shortstop and utility player for the Chicago Cubs. All Cub fans who listened to the radio broadcasts before and during the early days of Ernie Banks, remembered Smalley, not as the father of Roy Smalley, Jr., (who turned out statistically much better than his father) but as the greatest infielder the Cubs ever had-at least until the last inning of tight games.

Probably one of the reasons the Cubs had not been in the World Series since 1945, rather than the mid 50's, was because Roy Smalley somewhat routinely booted in the winning runs for the opposition after making spectacular play after play throughout the earlier innings of the game. Obviously this was not the fault of Smalley who couldn't produce in the late innings, but it was a management problem for failing to replace him at the white knuckle time of the game. But those were the days of player coaches like Phil Caveretta and the infamous college of coaches for the Cubs which had a rotating staff of coach of the month. Under those circumstances, the Cubs management was obviously preoccupied with other functions than managing the players on the field.

At any rate, Rex was a distant, but bona fide relative of a major leaguer, something no one else in or around Sam Hill could claim. A few of the old timers in Sam Hill claimed that their wives or sisters had dated Bob Feller while he was still in school up the road at Van Meter. But so many people had made this claim that if the Indian fireball specialist had taken the time to date or even visit with the wives or sisters of the claimants, rapid Robert would have spent twenty four hours a day with the women and would not have had time to lift, let alone throw, a baseball until he would have been about forty-seven years old.

Rex not only claimed a distant relationship to a major leaguer, but a few of those special genes that are gifted to athletes capable of playing professional baseball were passed to Rex as evidence of his heritage and he was captain of three sports during his senior year in high school.

Rex had gone to Sam Hill Junior College but never finished. He gave up his potential career in sports for the young and hot blooded Roseanne Cataloni, the Italian Des Moines girl who sat behind him in modern history. She occasional rubbed his back with her pencil. When the teacher was at the blackboard she whispered crude and corruptive messages to him so she could watch his ears turn red and the dark locks of his curly hair on his neckline straighten and stand on end. Often, as they left class, she would hand him notes to arouse the prurient interests within his inexperienced boyhood, and she guffawed and delighted as he would stumble out of the room clutching her missives of ardor.

Before the semester ended, Rex and Roseanne walked that fateful mile down the aisle and after passing up a scholarship to the University of Iowa, Rex found himself working sixty hours per week at the packing plant on the edge of town. From there he had nowhere to go beyond the assembly line and each day of living with Roseanne gave him the uncomfortable thought that he actually preferred the wretched assembly line as opposed to being with her.

Recently, Rex had received a bonus at work. It was not really a bonus or a raise, but the union steward called it a fringe benefit of great importance. It was a $100,000 life insurance policy which Rex never could have gotten for himself except that it was a group policy with open enrollment which meant the insurance company had to accept all applicants. There was a double indemnity provision for accidental death but a two year exclusion of any benefits in the event of suicide. Roseanne was not happy about this wonderful fringe benefit because it had no cash value to pay all of the past due bills which she had incurred.

Theirs was a traditional marriage. Rex worked sixty hours per week at the packing plant and Roseanne plotted, planned and devoted sixty hours per week toward spending more than Rex made. Most of the remaining 108 hours per week were spent with Roseanne yelling and screaming at Rex to get a better job or find a second job so that they could make ends meet. Rex was compelled to consult an attorney about a possible bankruptcy. Bankruptcy was considered morally reprehensible to nearly everyone in Sam Hill. The names of bankrupt petitioners were put in the paper and even during the farm crisis a few years back, the race to the bankruptcy courthouse did not involve any participants that Rex knew or associated with. After being counselled by the attorney as to the lack of alternatives to filing bankruptcy, Rex decided what he had to do. He recalled Carl Carlson's stories about sharks killing swimmers and frequent drownings in the waters of the Pacific. He decided to borrow his remaining limits from the friendly, overextending credit union and he would then go away and accidentally die so the policy would pay two hundred grand. Roseanne's bills would be paid and she would have enough left over to live comfortably without having to search for another man to sponge off and make miserable.

Rex opened his eyes. The thoughts of his pleasant childhood memories and dreams had been replaced by the sadness of his adulthood. His feet were exploding within the loafers, but he could do nothing about it except wonder if in fact he was wearing the loafers or whether it was the moccasins or the slippers.

Rex picked up the paperback book that Charity had given him, and began reading. It seemed to be a well written book and had some sort of miraculous sedative powers. Within a few minutes something occurred which had never happened to Rex Smalley before on an airplane. He was sound asleep.

A few minutes later the stewardess who could have been a ballet performer floated by. She gently lifted the book off the huge man's chest, and spread three blankets over him. She smiled and gently patted his large folded hands. She continued to float down the aisle to the coach section of the plane, where a distraught mother was unsuccessfully attempting to control a two year old with an ear infection and a disposition bent toward causing turmoil for every passenger within three rows.

Charity, gracefully rubbing the cover of the book with her long slender fingers, consoled the upset young mother and said, "Someone left this book on board several weeks ago and we discovered that anyone reading this becomes relaxed. You might try reading it to your youngster since it is written for a vast array of audiences, even though some newspaper reviews claim that it is meant for a cult type following. In either event it recently reached the New York Times top five listings."

The young mother looked at the book, and after studying the cover for a few minutes, smiled.

"Yes, it looks very interesting," she said to Charity, who smiled back and floated toward the first class area.

The mother then said to the toddler, "Look, darling, the nice lady has given us a children's book. See the cover where the brave man is bungee jumping from the hot air balloon toward the burning bridge."

A few minutes later the youngster was sleeping soundly in his mother's arms, and as both rested, neither heard the popping of leather stitching from the first class area.

46

BEACH BOUND

There was a slight drizzle in Honolulu as Rex deplaned. Even after moving around in the airport, the swelling feet continued to throb even though Rex had thrown away the ripped shoes and stepped into his sandals. While waiting at the carousel for his luggage, several preteen-aged Japanese boys approached Rex and held out paper and a pen to him. He tried to ignore them, but one of the parents of the youngsters then told him in broken English that the children perceived him as a great American sumo wrestler who would probably be victorious in the matches set in Blaisdell Auditorium over the weekend. Rex glared at the father and the children and they all stepped away and retreated to the other side of the carousel.

Huffing and puffing with his one suitcase and carry-on bag, Rex waited patiently as several empty taxis passed by him at the curb of the airport. He knew from experience that they were afraid he would do great damage to their shock absorbing systems so he waited in the mist until a public transportation bus stopped. He took the bus to the Waikiki area where he found a modest hotel which catered to transients. Two bellboys removed the cot from the small room which he rented and they put a king size mattress on the floor so that he could rest without fear of breaking the bed.

The mist had abated, but even with the overcast sky, the air was extremely warm. Even though it was well into the night hours at home, there was still over an hour of daylight so Rex decided to walk the beach. He had still not been able to formulate a fool proof method of doing away with himself and he thought that a walk on the beach might clear his head and allow him to think. He removed his shirt, grabbed a towel from the compact bathroom which appeared tiny when his huge frame filled its small dimensions, and from there he waddled toward the beach.

Rex did not have time to think about his problems once he reached the beach. Waikiki is not only the most crowded beach in the world on nice days, but even on cloudy days the beach leaves little room for movement. Rex had to concentrate very hard to walk around and through the mass of bodies which occupied the beach all the way from the Hilton to the area across from Kapioloni Park. The sand ground against the bottom of his feet like sandpaper and was extremely bothersome in the areas where the skin had stretched so much that it had ripped and was oozing blood. Nonetheless, he persevered onward to take in as many sights as possible to put in his memory bank which of course would not be needed in a few days.

After a few hundred yards, Rex was completely out of breath and needed to stop. He was afraid to sit down because he did not know if he would be able to get back up. He stood and gazed at the ocean which was filled with cargo ships, tourist boats and small craft including catamarans and crew boats. For each lazy, tanning beach bound worshiper of the sun which wasn't even shining, there was another person energized and moving in synch with the ebb and flow of the Pacific waters.

While Rex was tacitly making these observations, he heard giggling behind him. He slowly turned and looked down where a couple were trying to contain their laughter. Rex tried to stare menacingly at them but slowly it dawned on him that they were not laughing at him. The young man had a crew cut and tattoo of an anchor and eagle on his biceps. It was clear that he was a proud marine and his girlfriend or wife was a beautiful Asian with long black hair and a natural tan. The girl, after controlling her laughter, held a book close to her face and then read to her lover in a language that Rex guessed was Fijian or Tahitian. She could barely get out a sentence or two without nearly going into convulsions. The tough looking young marine was giggling so hard tears were running down his cheek. They were oblivious to Rex. Before Rex turned and started back to his room, he squinted closely at the book that she was reading. On the cover was a picture of a man bungee jumping from a hot air balloon toward a burning bridge.

47

THE VISIONARY

That night Rex could not sleep so he walked the Waikiki streets gazing in the various shops and watching the horde of American and Japanese shoppers as they hustled from store to store with their plastic sacks of keepsakes. Rex found a sturdy looking bench on the edge of the sidewalk in front of the International Marketplace and there he plopped his weary body with a thump. He watched the scurrying crowd for a few minutes and after heaving a large sigh, he let his heavy eyelids close for a moment.

When he opened his eyes again he noticed that the bench had another occupant. He looked to his right and saw a beautiful thin blonde removing a spiked heel and rubbing a thin ankle with her long narrow fingers. His eyes wandered up her long slender legs and saw that the black leather skirt stopped a few inches below her waist. Her blouse was made of matching black leather and when his gaze reached her face, he was shocked to realize that it was the ballerina stewardess, Charity. As he stared at her, she glanced at him and moved her eyes up and down the street looking for someone to return her look and lock into her eyes.

Rex furrowed his eyebrows and said to her, "Excuse me, but is your name Charity?"

She moved her eyes back in his direction and, without pity or shame, she unabashedly reviewed his enormity. Without showing any expression or emotion, she simply replied, "No, I'm Hope."

Although this was not what she had in mind, her eyes and Rex's eyes were locked in on each other. Slowly she smiled. Rex did not know what to do but thought he should at least try to make a conversation. Not knowing what else to say, he then pressed forward. "Do you have a twin sister named Charity, because I thought I met you earlier, and this young woman looks identical to you."

Part of Hope's business success hinged on the initial eye contact and she noticed that Rex had not yet blinked. She raised her eyelids and concentrated on making him blink first. However, the mutual staring continued while there was a long pause before she answered. Finally, she said, still without blinking, "I do not have a twin sister."

A charter fishing boat captain who was looking for potential customers for the next day's adventure was standing beside their bench when the eyes locked in. Before the next words were spoken and before Rex finally blinked and broke the spell, the captain was two blocks away where he was trying to pull in his catch for the night, two love struck honeymooners who were afraid to admit to him that their preference would be to spend the next day in their room with the Do Not Disturb sign insuring their privacy.

Rex wanted to continue to look at this extraordinary woman of the night, but his Lutheran background and small town upbringing caused him to turn his head away from her. Hope knew that she had until morning to bring happiness and joy to those seeking her companionship, so she reinitiated the conversation with the distraught giant. "I am sure I would have recognized you if you had been in town for long. Where are you from and how long are you going to be here in Oahu ?" she asked.

Rex twisted his body slightly and turned his neck so that he could again feast upon her. He then told her where he lived and worked, but he was cautious not to share his problems for fear that she would find him disgusting and would get up and leave rather than be brought into his murk and mire. He felt it would be safe to share with her the unusual ability to have visions that he had inherited from his father.

Rex's father was much luckier than Rex had been. His father had finished his education and played a couple years semi-pro baseball before settling down with a first rate woman who bore him three children, the middle child being Rex. His dad never seemed to work hard, but always maintained a living sufficient enough to supply the staples for the family. Some people said the old man was just plain lucky, sometimes, but he confided to Rex that there was a special gift that he had and that it was apparent that Rex was the only one of his children who had propensities for the gift.

Rex's father had the foresight to invest in AT&T stock in the 30's and although that was his most recognized piece of good luck, Rex and the other family members all knew when dad needed money he could go to the commodity broker and within a few days there was always a refurbished bank account.

As Rex got older, he realized that this gift that his father had was not bestowed exactly the same way to him. He was unable to predict the landing of the dice, and had no feel for the stock market. However, Rex did see things days, months and sometimes years before the rest of the world.

The first time that Rex was aware of this gift was when he was writing an essay in eighth grade. His research books on Niagara Falls indicated that a total of eight men had defied death by going over the falls in a barrel. His teacher double checked the subject and lowered Rex's grade for faulty research because only seven men had accomplished the feat. Rex went back and reread his research books and sure enough, where he had written down number eight and even given a name, the books showed nothing. The following autumn Rex heard the morning coffee drinkers at Soupys discussing the latest miracle at Niagara Falls, even confirming by name the person that Rex had discussed in his paper.

Rex's prescience occurred at least once a year. The last time was when Rex saw on CNN news that a devastating earthquake had struck California. There had been no deaths because the quake had hit during the early morning hours of a holiday and the highways which crumbled were mostly vacant. When Rex discussed this with Roseanne the next morning she accused him of being on hallucinatory substances and it was not until Rex was making his plans to kill himself that the earthquake actually rocked southern California at

3:00 a.m. on Martin Luther King's birthday.

Hope listened to Rex intently and then she said to him, "This is all very interesting, but it is obvious that you have a very serious problem. I am willing to listen for a few minutes if you would be unafraid to share this with me."

She recrossed her legs and while slipping off the second spiked shoe with her right hand, her left hand extended along the top of the bench until it lightly came to rest on Rex's right shoulder.

Rex swallowed hard, closed his eyes and after taking a deep breath, looked back at her. Slowly it started to come out. Then as the pent up hurt and anger released itself with each harsh statement, the words came out faster causing emotional weight to fall from his mouth.

The repressed memories of Roseanne's solutions to disagreements burst from the recesses of his memory and flowed out his mouth. He revisited the night that Roseanne caused an electrical outage by throwing a lamp at him which was still plugged in the wall socket. He recalled the evening when he returned from work to see his clothes flying through the air out of his bedroom window. He told of several incidents in restaurants in Des Moines when Roseanne threw food and hot coffee on him during her frequent tantrums.

As he spoke, he could feel Hope's fingernails digging into his right shoulder. The touching and probing of her fingers caused more of the memories to surface. He recollected the times that he told Roseanne, in frustration, that their unhealthy situation must end and each time that he would attempt this, she would counter with feigned attempts at suicide to prevent him from leaving.

He remembered the full bottle of aspirin which was always kept handy and the two occasions when he put his finger down her throat to induce vomiting the handfuls of aspirin that she had taken. He recalled feeling guilty because there was an instant when he wanted to remove his finger from her throat and allow the overdosing substance to remain and do its work. The confessions and recollections continued to pour. He related to Hope the time that Roseanne had put the knife to her wrist and when he made no effort to stop her, she lunged at him causing a cut on his rib area which scarred and expanded as his body ballooned over the years.

Then, the final and deepest hurt came out. Rex's voice cracked as he told how Roseanne had intentionally fallen down the stairs of their apartment and after this unsuccessful attempt to abort their only child, she waited until the following weekend and as Rex thought they were enjoying a Sundays outing in the car, she opened her passenger door and leaped into a ditch which succeeded in depriving him of the one child that they conceived.

After this final revelation, Rex realized that he was exhausted. Slowly, Hope removed her hand from his shoulder and unlocked the eye contact which she had maintained during his disclosures.

Rex felt a great relief sweep over his entire frame. He sighed heavily and watched as Hope lit a cigarette and smoked in silence. After she finished her cigarette, Hope slipped her shoes back on and assured Rex that things would be better. For some reason, he actually felt better already and thanked her for listening to him.

She stood up and started gazing at the crowd which continued to scurry by. A young Hawaiian man who was visiting Oahu for the sumo championships stopped a few feet away. He stared at Hope and when their eyes met, hers seared through him like a magnet and he could not turn away. Her lips formed two words and he could see the soft gush of air blow the words from her mouth toward his ears.

Rex was watching the exchange and saw the words escaping. They were "wela ule?"

Rex saw the young man's face turn crimson and noticed goose bumps appearing on the young Hawaiian's arms. The young Hawaiian then replied with the following response, "wela kohe?"

Still maintaining the locked eye contact, Hope nodded to the Hawaiian and glided to him. He put his arm through hers and as he led her down the street, Rex noticed how she floated rather than walked away.

Rex was famished after the exchange with Hope. He stopped at an open air restaurant and ordered several additional scoops of rice with the pua`a, which he discovered was pork.

While he was eating he listened to the commentator on the television which the employees at the Japanese restaurant were watching during slow periods. The first item on the news was concerning the early results of the sumo wrestling tournament. The next item concerned the heroic efforts which were going on in Maui to save a pregnant humpback whale which somehow became beached in shallow waters after seeking the low waters to deliver its baby. The broadcaster mentioned that the whale was surrounded by over a dozen sharks, causing a perilous situation. Excited marine biologists were shown to the viewers. One was extremely excited because it was hoped that the whale would actually give birth while still stranded, which is an event that has never been witnessed by human beings.

The few other people who were watching the telecast turned and discussed these local interest topics amongst themselves while Rex continued to gaze at the television. The last story concerned negotiations between *Time* magazine and the owner of a video cassette which reportedly showed clearly the grassy knoll area in Dealey Plaza at the time President Kennedy was being assassinated. Although no final purchase had yet been made by the magazine, the latest offer was one million dollars.

48

SHAVED ICE & SHARKS

The next morning did not start well for Rex. The manager of the hotel had removed the furniture so the bellboys could place the oversized mattress down. Rex was used to holding on to his night table and pulling himself out of bed and on this day he had nothing to grab. He rolled to the door and found he was able to grab the door handle and eventually he raised himself to his feet.

He lathered the left side of his face and standing before the mirror, he began shaving. After finishing, he lathered the right side and then moved to his left. He could then see the right side of his body in the mirror, which like his mirror at home, was only wide enough for half of him at one time.

While shaving his right side, he noticed the raspberry colored mark on his right shoulder. Looking more closely at it, he saw that there was a discoloration of the skin where Hope had touched him the night before. This discoloration was slightly warm to the touch, but otherwise there appeared to be no change in his body. However, the strange sensation of lightness in his mind that he had felt the night before still lingered.

Rex knew that the beaches on this crowded island were not known for shark attacks and if he were to make himself available as shark bait, he probably should go to Maui where the sharks were apparently plentiful, since they were surrounding the beached whale. On the bus to the airport, he found himself signing several autographs for youngsters who were sumo fans.

While he was purchasing his one way ticket to Maui at the Aloha Airlines desk, Rex heard a college aged boy making fat jokes about him in an effort to impress his girlfriend. One of the comments was that the mother of Gilbert Grape would have looked skinny next to the man buying his ticket. Rex did not turn around, but he did want to put the young man in his place. He could have told the young gawkers that even though the town of Endora was two counties away from Sam Hill, Rex knew the Grape family and had played high school baseball against Gilbert's father. At that time Gilbert's mother was not only lean, but she was beautiful and if she and Rex had stood side by side a quarter of a century ago, the picture would have made any swimwear magazine. However, it was sour Grapes to go into the past. The Grapes were now dead and soon Rex would be also.

When he arrived in Maui, Rex rented a car so he could find a fairly secluded beach where there might be hungry sharks waiting for him. He headed toward Lahaina but first turned southeast toward Makena. Finding no suitable shark waters near Makena or Wailea, he returned and drove through the town of Kehei. The main street had interesting looking stores on one side while the beach on the ocean-side looked perfect.

He parked the car and made a closer examination of the beach, finding that even on clear, warm, beautiful days such as this one was becoming, there were very few people actually on the beach. This would be best so that when the sharks attacked, there would be a lesser chance that he would be rescued before being torn apart by the razor sharp jaws of death. As he thought about his body being dismembered, his throat parched.

He crossed the street to Pilialoha's Shaved Ice and Ice Cream Shop. This was literally a grass hut built on a raised wooden floor about two steps above the sand ground. Even though it was lunch time, only one customer was in the hut which had modern ice cream freezers that were decorated with palm tree branches in such a manner as to cover the units except for the glass showcase which presented the various flavors of ice cream.

Rex immediately knew he was interrupting a rather heated conversation between the beautiful young Hawaiian girl and the old man who appeared to be of Chinese extraction. Part of the conversation was interspersed with Hawaiian words, but it was obvious to Rex that the girl must be Pilialoha, the owner of the store, and the older man was the owner of the sandy realty. Apparently Pilialoha was delinquent in her rent payments and the landlord was threatening to take a bulldozer to her little grass hut ice cream and shaved ice parlor, while she was begging for additional time to increase her business. When the old man saw Rex covering the entrance, he quit talking and left after Rex moved forward to make room.

Pilialoha sold Rex a triple root beer float and two scoops of rainbow flavored shaved ice. While he was quenching the tightness in his throat with this snack, Pilialoha told him many things about the island and about her family.

Her last name was Tyler and her great-grandfather Tyler, a non kama`aina, had settled as a missionary on Maui around the turn of the century. All of her other family members were one hundred percent Hawaiian natives. She and her brother were the first two to leave the islands as they both went to San Diego State for college. She had returned home two years ago and her father had recently built the shack not knowing that the landlord, who indeed was Pake, or Chinese, would raise the rent each month as her little business grew.

They had no written lease and the whole thing was getting pupule! Whenever she thought about it she became huhu wela loa. Rex explained to her that he could not understand the Hawaiian words so she told him that this whole business with the landlord was crazy and made her extremely angry. She became so excited in her conversation with Rex that she immediately forgot what he said and she then told him that there was very little that could be done with he kanaka ikaika. After Rex shrugged, she realized another interpretation was necessary so she told him in English that the Chinaman was a very powerful person and that eventually she would probably lose her business.

Rex then asked her if the beach across the street contained many sharks. She looked at him as if she had not heard him properly and she queried, "Mano?"

Rex again shrugged and she said, "Did you say sharks?"

Now that they were back to English, the conversation went more quickly and she assured him that the beach was very safe and there had been no sharks in these waters for many years. Rex asked her where the beached humpback whale was because he heard there had been sharks in that area, but Pilialoha said she was unaware of any whale problems. However, he probably should go up to Lahaina and check out the whale sighting boats which were docked behind the Pioneer Hotel. They would have all the information on any beached whales. She then bid him mahalo as he grunted and groaned while taking the two steps down to the sand terrain which was owned by the nasty Chinaman.

In less than an hour Rex was standing on the dock watching the fishing boats and whale watching boats as they gathered their adventure seeking tourists. He had taken a few minutes to view the banyan tree across the street which was reported to be the largest in the world. It was rather an awesome tree as its branches spread out to cover more than the area of a city block. The park area which contained the tree was mostly in shade. Rex had felt a sort of rapport with the tree, but realized that he had business to attend, so he left the mighty tree and went to the boat dock.

None of the captains were aware of a beached whale, so Rex found the largest boat and bought a ticket for a three hour whale watch. The captain was concerned about possible rocking of the boat causing sea sickness to the other approximate one hundred customers, so he asked Rex to position himself exactly in the middle of the ship.

Several whales were seen as the ship traversed the area between Maui and Moloka`i. One of the baby whales playfully came within a few yards of the snapshot happy group. The captain advised his tour group that the baby's sole source of food was from the mother and that the large adult whales ate nothing from the time they migrated from the Arctic waters until they would return several months later.

The adults would weigh as much as forty tons and after the babies were born, they could gain as much as several hundred pounds per day from the feedings supplied by the mother whales. This information did not make Rex happy. Here these monsters went months without eating and they still were huge. There was absolutely no hope for him because he could not stand even going a few hours without some sort of feeding.

As they were heading back toward the dock, Rex saw the beached whale. It was very far away and appeared to be stuck on a rocky miniature island that was probably a couple hundred yards from shore. He tried to tell the captain of the sighting and even yelled the traditional "Thar she blows" but the captain ignored him. It was only when Rex threatened to walk to the side of the boat that the captain agreed to go in for a closer look.

The captain was truly amazed to see the large whale so close to shore and completely beached on the area where silt had built up to the point that it actually created a tiny island. While all of the customers were excitedly taking pictures and the captain was radioing to the shore patrol, Rex looked not at the whale, but at the surrounding water for shark fins to be cutting through the top of the water. When the captain navigated the vessel close to the unhappy whale, Rex asked the captain about the potential for sharks. The captain gave Rex a strange look and told him that there were no sharks in these waters.

Rex knew better because he had never been wrong in his visions. He decided to slip and fall over the side as soon as the sharks appeared.

A few minutes later the area was converged with divers, marine biologists and other whale watching vessels. Everyone watched as divers and aquatic specialists entered the waters and approached the huge mammal to determine how to save it. Rex noticed that several of the divers had an insignia sewn on to their wet suits. He squinted to make out the logo and then realized that the red lettering said "Honolulu Sharks". He turned to the captain and asked what the deal was with the divers and their insignia. The captain then told him that the professional winter baseball season had just ended and some of the players were staying through the winter. They were being paid by the state to work on rescue units, and yes, the name of one of the baseball teams is the Honolulu Sharks.

49

MEETING TYLER TYLER

Rex realized that he probably would not be eaten by a shark at Maui. The big island might provide better opportunities for an accident. It offered steep volcanic cliffs and a better possibility of being attacked by hungry sharks. Also, Oahu and Maui were too beautiful to desecrate by doing the deed that he knew must be done. Perhaps the island of Hawaii would be more acceptable for his rendezvous with fate.

Rex checked the airline's schedule to the big island and then looked at his watch. He had purchased the Seiko about eight years before, and it was wonderful for making sure he was always at work at time. He had taken great pride in the fact that his punch card indicated that he was never late for work.

The day after he bought the watch, he realized that it was running five minutes fast. After setting it back, he monitored the watch for the next week and every day, he found that it was five minutes fast. He had considered returning the time piece to the Ben Franklin store, but he was on the shift that coincided with the hours at Ben Franklin, so it seemed easier just to reset it each day. One weekend he forgot to check the watch and found, after neglecting to reset it for three days, that it was still only five minutes fast. He started checking the watch only weekly and eventually monthly, and to his amazement he discovered that every time he reset the watch, it would run ahead five minutes during the first day, but thereafter would keep perfect time so that it was always only five minutes fast!

It turned out to be the best watch he'd ever owned. He could be a few minutes late and still be early or at least on time and he never had to reset the watch unless he was bored and wanted something to do.

185

Rex was beginning to realize that other than for plane schedules, there was not a great deal of need for a timepiece on the islands. People tended to eat when they were hungry, sleep when they were tired, and very few jobs required exact hours.

He imagined that the military personnel on the bases probably were required to live by the clock, but even the soldiers appeared unaware of the necessity of time when he observed them, which was of course while they were away from their military environment.

Rex took Hawaiian Airlines to the Hilo side of the island. He rented a car and drove to the national forest where a volcano was actively pouring lava over the side of a cliff into the ocean. He spent a few hours watching this majestic display of nature.

The red hot flow would gently stream from the bowels of the mountain with an occasional gust of energy which would cause the molten mass to jump into the air and fly over the edge of the cliff, where it would smash into the pounding sea causing a loud hiss at the moment of collision. The ocean was intent on exterminating the heat from the lava flow while the steaming lava seemed equally determined to push back the sea and increase the land mass. The struggle was intense, but Rex sensed that eventually the mountain would gasp its last hot breath and the war would eventually be won by the ocean which would never give up. However, until that time, the battle was being won by the volcano since the size of the island was increasing each year through this majestic process.

Rex briefly contemplated walking into the lava flow, but he could not seriously contemplate the pain that would be associated with being melted by the burning cinders. Rex had been warned that the Hilo side of the island was subject to damp and rainy weather, and when the dark rain cloud covered the volcanic area, Rex retreated and headed for the Kona side of the island where he knew there were be more sunshine and perhaps the place to find an accident which would not burn or hurt terribly while causing his death.

Unfortunately, Rex found the town of Kailua-Kona to be similar to the other island towns he had visited. Honolulu had been bustling and metropolitan, but the other places were all much more laid back, unassuming, and even in a vague way reminiscent of the small town from which he had escaped. The pier near the center of the town provided some swimming area, but since there were no sand beaches, the number of people in and around the water was very miniscule compared to Waikiki.

Rex had the foresight to bring his home made swimming suit with him since he knew that none of the shops would carry a suit large enough for him. It was basically a conglomerate of towels that had been sewn together by some of the ladies in Edna's nursing home.

He waddled to the end of the pier and fell into the ocean. The splash created a surfer's delight for those who had been waiting all day for the perfect wave. Rex pushed himself away from the pier and bobbed up and down, slowly moving further into the salty brine.

Within a few minutes Rex was exhausted. This could be it. Perfect. He knew that if there were no sharks in the area he probably would still be unable to return to shore because he had expended so much energy pushing himself outward. However, the tide was pulling him inward and in order to avoid being pushed back to the shoreline, he continued to use all of his remaining energies fighting for deeper waters.

His natural buoyancy, coupled with the salt water, made it impossible for his head to go under. He bobbed up and down until his skin was completely waterlogged. He waited and waited, but nothing happened. His body continued to bob. Eventually, the sun dropped behind the horizon and even though Rex realized this was the most beautiful sunset he had ever seen, he felt frustrated as the shoreline became shadowy. He could see the town become artificially illuminated as the restaurants and shop owners used electrical power to replace the natural power of the sun. The sea calmed itself and Rex stopped bobbing. His body was now motionless, several hundred yards from the shore.

He was amazed at how far sounds would travel on the now quiet water. He could hear lovers and parents as they walked along the street bordering the ocean. He could even hear the sounds of pebbles skipping across the water as children relished in the afterglow of day. He even heard fisherman on the pier singing a song he hadn't heard for years. It was the sad ballad of Clementine.

Rex heard a sound that was becoming familiar to him after being on the islands a few days. A small rowboat was passing close by him and the sounds of the oars moving against the water became louder and louder. Suddenly, he felt a lasso being thrown over his body and a voice called out telling him to hold onto the rope. The next thing he knew, he was being pulled through the water back towards shore. It made him think of the story by Hemingway in which the huge giant fish was being towed by the old man. He wondered if the sharks would now come and tear his body away as they did in that wonderful story. Such was not to be the case on this night, however, and within a few minutes he found himself back at the pier where the young Hawaiian in the rowboat was pulling him out of the water.

Rex was mildly surprised when the young man acted as though this were an every day occurrence. Several large blankets were taken from the rowboat and given to Rex to use as a towel. The young man gave him some puu puu to eat and then provided some beef and cream which Hawaiians call pipi kalima. Seeing that Rex was still hungry, the young man volunteered his remaining food, which he described as hua, though the huge man recognized this as five eggs.

After taking the edge off his ravenous hunger, Rex went to the small beach area next the pier and rested. It was only then that he felt like talking to the young man who had pulled him away from what would have been a long and cold night of bobbing up and down in the ocean a few hundred yards from the shore.

"Aloha, my friend. I probably would not have been able to drown out there, so I do owe you for bringing me in. What is your name?" Rex asked.

"I go by Tyler" the young man said while busying himself with the gutting and cleaning of the fish that he had caught.

"What is your last name, Tyler?" Rex asked, expecting the young man to furnish him with an unpronounceable medley of double vowels.

"Tyler."

Rex said, "I'm sorry, Tyler, I thought you meant your first name was Tyler. What is your first name?"

"Tyler."

For the next few minutes, the only sound was that of the sharp knife gutting the fish and filleting the meat. Rex needed time to think this out. Finally, Rex tried again.

"Tyler, am I correct in understanding that both your first name and last name is Tyler?"

The young man stopped his work and while still squatting, turned toward Rex and said, "Tyler Tyler is a redundancy. No one calls me that. Everyone just calls me Tyler, except for the old man who works at the bait shop. He stutters very badly and he cannot help but call me Tyler Tyler."

There was another silence as the Hawaiian finished filleting the last fish.

Rex took a deep breath and said, "Tyler, this may sound strange to you. It seems that everyone I converse with on these islands ends up with me asking them the same question. I hope this doesn't bother you, but I met a girl in Maui named Tyler and I wonder if she could be your sister."

The young man stood up and threw the fish entrails into the ocean and packed the meat into a burlap bag. He turned to Rex, shrugged his shoulders and replied, "I don't have any sisters who go by Tyler. But I do have a sister in Maui whose name is Pelialoha, which means beloved relative. You see, it is our custom to call each other only by our first name and we feel offended if someone addresses us otherwise."

Rex, from his sitting position, looked up at Tyler and said, "I think I understand."

As Tyler was gathering his fishing equipment and securing his rowboat to the pier, Rex learned that Tyler, like his sister, Pelialoha, was an entrepreneur. Tyler had a small book store in the mini mall about a block from the pier and he assured Rex that if he needed some part-time work, there was a clerk's job available in the bookstore.

That night Rex slept on the floor at one of the many chapels in the area. Although several other transients were also resting in the chapel, Rex's sleep was disturbed because throughout the night the natives would enter the building, pause to light a few candles and murmur prayers of thanksgiving and petitions of concern.

While one of the faithful was visiting with her creator, Rex dreamed. He saw Roseanne in the basement of the courthouse in Sam Hill. The jailer had locked her in and the keys were on the floor several feet beyond her reach. He could hear her piercing whiny voice calling his name over and over and over again. When he did not appear to her, she cursed him and spat on the floor of the cell. Her saliva and tears had filled her cell to the point that she was required to swim in the bodily fluids to avoid drowning. He hands were clutching the iron bars which separated her from freedom. She was kicking her feet in a frenzy to keep from slipping under the frothy liquid. As the dream faded away, the last thing Rex could see was the hatred in her eye as she stared at him on the other side of the bars where he stood completely dry.

The next morning Rex walked from the chapel to one of the open windowed restaurants which overlooked the ocean. He saw several joggers and bicyclists as they toned up their bodies and dispensed with excess calories. It dawned on him that since he probably could not drown in the salty water and since he was not appealing to the man eating fish, perhaps a little exercise might just do him in. After eating a hearty breakfast, he decided to run the streets like the other joggers and within a few minutes he would probably be corpus delicti.

He moved one foot in front of the other. He had not moved his legs so fast in some time and immediately he broke into a sweat. He was a little disappointed to see pregnant women who were out for a walk speed by him. What was especially disheartening was that he and they were going in the same direction. However, he kept moving his legs and tried to keep in mind that everything was relative. What was a crawling pace for many people was a flat out sprint for Rex. The sweat continued to break throughout his body until he felt that he was back in the ocean. He continued to push on until his breath was completely depleted and his arms and legs ached and burned. He would have fallen, except there was a telephone pole which he grabbed. He could feel a rumble in his stomach and suddenly the breakfast that he had just consumed was splashing all over the pavement. Exhausted, he sat down and looked back to where he had started running. He had covered a total of 100 yards.

A few hours later, Rex decided to try it again, only without such a large amount of exertion initially. If he could maintain his running without becoming exhausted as quickly, there was a better chance that his heart would give out and he could have a nice quick explosion from within. This time he covered just over one-quarter of a mile before again grabbing another telephone pole in utter exhaustion. That evening, he made the third attempt at self-destruction and discovered that his body carried him almost half a mile. That night he was so tired that he did not hear the people as they entered and departed the chapel.

50

FAITH ON THE BIKE TRAIL

The next morning Rex decided he did not want to throw up again, so his breakfast was much lighter. His huge body had aches and pains in places that he did not know existed but he was determined to end it all on this day so that the aching would stop. Once again, morning, afternoon and evening he pushed his huge body up and down the street running along the coastline. Each time he would go slightly farther than the time before, and each time he thought he was coming nearer to the fatal heart attack which was inevitable.

On the third day, Rex heard the birds calling out to each other as they searched the ocean for food. He watched other joggers as they went past and even found himself nodding to a few of them. He even waved to two young girls who were engaged in deep conversation as they passed on the other side of the road.

It was on the eighth day that Rex realized that he was actually feeling better and that perhaps there might be an alternative to dying. That morning, he went to Tyler's bookstore and accepted a part-time job. As he jogged the mile and a half back to the chapel, he actually whistled and for the first time in a long time, felt the joy of living.

As he crested the final hill, he looked over the embankment to his right which ran to the ocean. He stopped and smelled the fragrances of tropical flowers growing along the roadway and in the volcanic rocks which jetted down to the ocean. He listened to the sounds of the water breaking against the cliffs. He gazed at the dazzling display of colors in the sky, ocean and lava fields. He was so absorbed in this that he did not hear the bicycle braking and he did not see the shocked look on the face of the young blond rider as she came over the hill on the pathway which his lumbering body was blocking.

He felt a bicycle bump against his left hip and the next thing he knew he was floating away from the path next to the road. His body was moving off the pathway and started floating toward the Pacific far below. He saw the startled look on the girl's face. She had a large cross on her neck which bounced from breast to breast in slow motion. Her long blond hair slowly bounced from side to side doing figure eights around her neck.

As gravity caught Rex and started pulling him downward, he wanted to open his mouth and ask the girl a question. He knew her. What was she doing here? She was supposed to be handing out favors to the young men in Waikiki. Or perhaps she was supposed to be comforting the passengers on the airplane. Was it Hope? Or Charity?

Suddenly, he felt his body as it scraped against the lava rocks which were piled high onto one another all the way down to the ocean. He felt himself tumbling, rolling, breaking and forfeiting the rest of his life. But before the pain and fear could set in, he yelled at the stunned girl who was now several yards above him, "Do you have a twin sister named Charity, or a twin named Hope?"

He could not hear an answer from her. He saw his watch smash against one of the jetting rocks. Time was standing still and he was slipping away into eternity. Two more bounces and he was gone.

Rex first thought that he was back in Sam Hill. He could not open his eyes, nor could he move. The first thing to come back was his hearing. The first words that he heard were as follows, "Paging Roger Klinker. Please report to the women's public rest room near the emergency room. Bring your mop and pail."

Rex did not know if it was seconds, minutes, hours or days later, but the next thing he heard was a doctor whispering to the nurse who was in charge of recording his chart. The doctor was telling her that the patient would soon die from his grossly obese size even if he recovered from the fall. The amazing thing was that he had lived long enough to have the unfortunate accident up on the cliff.

The next thing that Rex heard was the voice of another doctor who had apparently been examining him. The doctor must have been instructing several students at the time, because there was a good deal of laughter when the doctor said that there were not this many chins in a Chinese phone book. The last remark made Rex want to wake up so that such cruelty would stop. He forced himself into consciousness and opened his eyes.

Rex was lying on a large hammock. The bed had been taken from his room and this contraption was constructed so that the medical people could work on him without his excessive weight causing prohibitions on their work. He saw dozens of needles sticking throughout his body making him look like a porcupine. Attached to the needles were long tubes which ran to bags of fluids. There must have been 25 or 30 bags fastened to various locations near the ceiling. It looked like a circus with helium balloons floating everywhere. Rex could not move and as he started looking toward his body, he thought he saw a large cement building which encased him, then his eyes closed and he rested.

The next time Rex awoke, he saw the young blond with the cross standing next to his bed. She was holding his hand and smiling. The first thing she told him was that she and the other members of the mission had been praying for him continually since the accident seven weeks ago. The doctors had given little hope to this John Doe and she was convinced that God had answered their prayer and brought him safely back to them.

Rex was genuinely confused. For some reason he was happy not to be dead even though his only purpose in life was to kill himself. This made him a failure, but at least he was a happy failure, especially with this beautiful young woman holding his hand.

She looked at him and said, "You don't need to talk. Please preserve your strength. In case you were wondering, the answer to the question that you asked as you were falling, is no, I do not have any twin sisters named Charity or Hope. The only thing of importance now is that you know that my name is Faith. Although it sounds strange, I am a missionary, even though it is here in Hawaii. I was bicycling with other missionaries at the time of your accident. We bicycle the Word of God to people who can not be reached by motor vehicle. As converts are received, they will be trained to ride bicycles and spread the Word of God to others. In turn, they will teach their converts to spread the message by bicycle. Please get some rest and as soon as you get your strength back, we will take you to our mission home for further convalescence and rehabilitation."

Faith then turned and glided through the door, stopping to blow him a kiss and a goodbye with her long, slender white fingers.

Rex was not inclined to give the hospital staff his name, so he claimed amnesia. If they had notified Roseanne, she probably would have flown to Hawaii and then Rex would have been forced to again contemplate suicide. Since he was uninsured, the hospital exaggerated his recovery progress on his chart and as a result, within a few days he was released to Faith and her fellow missionaries.

Before he was discharged, one of the nurses remarked to Rex that when he was brought into the hospital, an attempt was made to weigh him. He was over the maximum on the hospital scales at that time and remarkably enough, a couple of days before he finally regained consciousness, he was weighed again and the scales still had 78 more pounds to register before going over the top. Rex was not sure if the nurse was trying to be nice to him or if she was telling the truth. However, he did notice that his clothing which Faith had retrieved from the chapel was, for the first time that he could remember, loose fitting.

He felt so good about all this that as he was leaving the hospital, he told the nurse that he knew what the doctor said about his life expectancy and that they just might be wrong. She said that she was unaware that any doctor had said anything to this affect, and that perhaps he had either been hallucinating or dreaming. Rex smiled at her and told her not to be embarrassed, but he really felt that he might prove them wrong. As he left the hospital, he actually skipped to the van which was owned by the mission and as they loaded him into the back of the van, he whistled something vaguely like Clementine while reviewing the hospital chart which they gave him. He was surprised to see that even though they had details of everything that went on during his hospitalization, including the fact that they noticed the red birth mark in the shape of a hand on his right shoulder, there was no mention of any heart failure or probable early death because of his weight.

As Faith drove away from the coastline toward the mission house nestled high in the lava fields, she turned on her cassette player. Her favorite Christian rock band, Petra, was singing their top hit, *The Sleeping Giant Gets a Wake-Up Call*. Rex was wondering where he could find another Seiko watch.

51

THE COMEBACK TRAIL

Rex spent the next few days resting and allowing the bruises which still permeated his body to heal. He wandered around the grounds belonging to the mission and Faith showed him the garden area which provided all the food for the students who lived on the premises.

Rex had been aware that the price of fruit on the islands was very expensive, so he was amazed to learn that it could grow abundantly in the lava enriched soil. The bananas were small, as were the oranges, but the guava was bountiful as was the mango fruit. There were hybrid fruits Rex had never tasted before including a milky mixture which seemed to be a cross between a pineapple and a banana. The vegetable garden provided the remaining necessities, other than the rice which was donated by one of the church affiliated groups which helped to sponsor the mission home and the individual student missionaries.

Some of the most beautiful flowers that Rex had ever seen were sprinkled throughout the grounds and Rex spent many of the daylight hours sitting under one of the kewei trees, looking at the rough but beautiful scenery and smelling the fragrances from the flowers and ripening food.

The mission had three full-time missionaries including Faith. Like her, the others were there for only a few months to help teach the students from the local Bible school who lived on the grounds and also prepare for their next mission. Faith was busy in corresponding with her sponsors as well as sharing in the daily chores of gathering and preparing the food and in her case, bicycling nearly 100 miles per day to prepare herself for her next mission field. Each evening after supper, there was extensive fellowship and Bible study and prayer sessions.

After a few days, Rex realized that there was no meat in the diet of anyone at the mission house and in fact, his food consumption was less than it had been for years. In spite of this, his energy level was increasing and he found himself taking longer and longer walks each day in addition to the increasing amount of time that he spent working in the garden.

Several of the students went into town each day for several hours to attend classes. Rex felt that he should contribute something financially and was pleasantly surprised to find out that Tyler would still give him part-time work at the bookstore. Thus, Rex found himself into a new and different routine than he had ever known. He was getting up early in the morning and walking and jogging before breakfast. He then worked several hours each day at the bookstore and returned in time to help gather supper and take another longer jog before the evening Bible study and prayers.

Several weeks after this routine, Rex made an amazing discovery. One day, after ringing up a sale at the bookstore, he dropped some change while handing it to a customer and to his utter amazement, he not only reached over and picked up the change, but after standing, he looked down and could actually see his feet. That evening at supper he mentioned this incident to Faith and she did admit that she had been periodically taking in his clothes so that they would not become too baggy on him.

It was not much later that he realized that he was no longer moving side to side when he shaved and his entire face was visible in the shaving mirror. As his body continued to lose it's massiveness, he even noticed that his nearly bald head was now growing long thick bundles of curly dark hair.

Each day he found renewed strength, which increased proportionately to the changes in his body. When he got to the point where his legs could straddle a bicycle, he started riding with Faith and was amazed at the number of miles that they could cover.

On the weekends, he started swimming to supplement the jogging and bicycling and instead of bobbing up and down in the water, he could feel his arms and legs kick and move and pull his ever constricting body along in fluid motion. His body had not reacted to these commands since his baseball playing days and Rex was truly amazed.

Rex knew from the calendar that winter had passed and the rest of the world which knew seasons was now well into spring. He thought about his past and Roseanne less and less. He had altered two of the numbers on his social security number when applying for the job with Tyler Tyler and he had told Tyler and everyone else that he met that his name was Rex King. His past was history and Rex Smalley no longer existed, but the new Rex King had emerged.

Several tri-athletes were living down the road from the mission. The Iron Man Triathlon is held every year in October. The event, which is carried worldwide on ESPN, is the most exacting of all physical endeavors. The first event is a two mile swim starting and finishing at the pier which is a short walk from Tyler's bookstore. After leaving the water, the participants jump on a bicycle for a 100 mile ride through the lava fields. At the end of the bicycle event, the athletes must then run a marathon. The most elite athletes in the world can finish this feat, including the 26-mile run, in somewhat over eight hours. Several of the top world class athletes had moved onto the island to do the last few months of training under the same conditions that would exist the day of the Iron Man competition.

Rex had watched with fascination as these athletes would work out each day. Their regimen would include at least six to eight hours of training. Initially, Rex would tag along behind them and see if he could keep up with their workouts for even a fraction of the time. He was surprised that his new physique would respond to the demands that were being placed upon it and by mid-summer, he decided to participate in an event which was still considered insane by most standards. It was the annual one-half Iron Man. Swim a mile. Bike for 50 miles. Run 13.1 miles.

The elite athletes left Rex and most of the other participants far behind. However, Rex was amazed to find that even though it was the most strenuous thing he had ever done, his body responded and he was able to finish. It took a full three days and a couple dozen aspirin to eliminate the aches and pains that were inflicted upon his muscles by the ordeal, but a natural high caused by the release of endocrines in his brain lasted longer than the fatigued muscles.

It was becoming apparent to Rex that if he continued to train, the Iron Man competition was possible. Throughout the rest of the summer and into the fall, Rex continued to push his body until he became convinced that he was capable of completing the most physically punishing sporting event in the world. By September, Rex could step on the bathroom scales and look down to see that the needle stopped at 224 lbs. He then pulled his head up and looked in the mirror to see in the reflection a body which contained less than 15% body fat and resembled the pictures he, as a child, had seen in magazines of that great weight lifter, Charles Atlas.

<h1 style="text-align:center">52</h1>

A REUNION AT WORK

Most of the money that Rex earned at Tyler's was given to the mission. However, he did make one small indulgence for himself. On each occasion that he passed a store which sold watches, he would try to find one which had the magical attributes of his previous watch. However, after weeks and weeks of futilely trying to find such a watch, he gave up and purchased one which kept exact time to the second and never ran fast or slow. He also realized that his powers to foretell events before their occurrence had disappeared as his new body had taken shape.

Rex could feel the excitement growing throughout the island as the countdown to the Iron Man Triathlon approached. In addition to the fervor that seemed to permeate the entire island, an additional excitement was exuded by both Tyler and Faith. Rex did not pay much attention to their excitement, but he did remember that Faith had told him that her sponsors would be arriving a few days before the triathlon. At about the same time, Tyler asked Rex to work a few extra hours because there was to be a book signing ceremony by a popular new author set for the weekend before the Iron Man.

Rex arrived early the day of the scheduled book signing, and he found that Tyler had already set up the booth and had several hundred books ready for autographing by the author. Rex cleaned up the rest of the store and set up other displays so that those who were waiting in line could perhaps pick out other works of literature.

Rex was in the back room doing inventory when the author arrived. As Rex came out to fill one of the shelves with the latest work by Phyllis Noble, he almost dropped the books. He had seen the author's name in copies of the book but it did not register with him until he saw Eric Erickson shaking hands with Tyler that Erickson was the same person he had remembered from Sam Hill.

Erickson glanced in his direction and waved, but there was no recognition, much the relief of Rex.

As Rex was recovering from his initial shock, a double jolt shot through his body as the door to the store opened and in walked a muscular middle-aged man with army fatigues and a floral printed shirt with a lei around his neck. Rex stepped backward and bumped into a shelf of books which nearly came crashing to the floor.

Barry Sardinhurst walked up to Tyler and shook hands as Eric patted Barry on the back and introduced him to Tyler.

Memories swept over Rex. He remembered the day that he and Herm Sherman had enlisted together under the buddy system. The Army kept its promise and sent both Herm and Rex to basic training and advanced infantry training together. They were even sent to Vietnam together where Herm was in charge of delivering mail to the Second/17th Artillery Battalion at An Khe. Rex was assigned to the same unit as a cook.

The first three months of their one-year commitment had been relatively quiet with only a few mortar attacks reminding them that they were in a war zone. Then one day after Herm finished the mail rounds, he went to the mess hall and told Rex that another of their high school buddies, Johnny St. Gerald, who was a warrant officer and pilot on helicopters which defoliated the region, would be at their camp a few days. The Saint's helicopter needed repairs which were being done in An Khe and this grounded him with them for several days.

When it came to time to test fly his helicopter, the Saint invited Herm and Rex along. They flew out and over the village which was just outside the main camp. The Saint suggested that they should check and see what some of the local papasans were doing. Herm and Rex stared blankly at each other, not knowing what Saint meant. Then, laughing, the Saint lowered the helicopter over one of the peasant homes. As he hovered over the house, he increased the velocity of the blades and as he did, the propellers forced a torrent of wind upon the grassy roof. Rex and Herm stood on each side of the helicopter and stared as the roof literally blew off the hut. Sure enough, a very old papasan was lying on a hammock smoking a pipe and staring blankly upward at them. Meanwhile, the old mamasan was running in from the rice paddy shaking her fist and screaming Vietnamese obscenities at the occupants of the helicopter.

The Saint then said that the other seven huts which were in a row needed to also be aired out and one by one, he negotiated the helicopter over each hut and blew their roofs off. Herm and Rex were so excited by the event that they could not control their bladders. They stood at the open doors of the helicopter and watched as their streams of urine turned into a misty yellow spray as the strong wind created by the whirling blade thrust it downward.

That night, their camp was barraged with mortars to such an extent that even the short timers could not remember such an attack. The Saint decided he should be back with his own unit and early the next morning, he took his helicopter and left. It was that afternoon, when Herm was out delivering mail to the battery located six miles east of the base camp that both he and the driver of his jeep disappeared. Much later, it was confirmed that he had been taken a prisoner of war and eventually he was rescued by Barry Sardinhurst.

Over the ensuing years, the Saint and Rex had worked together at the packing plant but never discussed the reunion in Vietnam. It was especially unpleasant each time that Herm would come home on furlough and stop to visit the Saint. The Saint's health had deteriorated slowly and steadily ever since they had returned from Vietnam and it was finally determined that he was suffering from too much exposure to Agent Orange, which was the primary defoliant that he used. Rex was almost thankful the day that the Saint had to quit work and went to the hospital for the last time.

Now, staring at Sardinhurst, Rex again felt the guilt that he had at the Saint's funeral, because instead of grieving that he lost a friend, Rex had in fact felt relieved at the death of the Saint, knowing that the reason Herm was captured would probably never be known.

Tyler called Rex to the front of the store and introduced Eric and Barry to Rex King. Eric was pre-occupied with making sure he had enough pens for the signatures and he merely gave a wave in Rex's direction. Barry, however, extended a strong right hand and stared directly into Rex's eyes as the two physical titans squeezed each other's hands.

The honking horn from a bus caused Barry to turn away. Tyler, Barry, Eric and Rex all looked out the front window and saw Faith emerging from a Roberts tour bus. She waved at them and then stood to help her sponsors off the bus.

For the third time in less than ten minutes, Rex nearly fainted. As the purple haired old ladies debarked from the bus, Rex realized that the sponsor for Faith was the Dorcas Society of Sam Hill. He recognized each and every one of them as they got off. There was Marie Witherspoon, Eleanor Sardinhurst, Valerie Salmon, Lillian Marshall, Elsie Campbell, Sophie Peck, Esther Ullestad and finally, Edna Grover. When Edna got off, Rex thought to himself that Barry's wife, Rachel, would not be there since she would be taking care of the patients at Edna's home. However, there was still a possibility that each and every one of these women could identify him.

As they helped each other, arm in arm, walking across the sidewalk toward the bookstore, an audible groan came forth from Rex. Also getting off the bus, but turning in a different direction were three more people. One was Herm Sherman. The second was a young man who worked at the corner restaurant. Rex thought it was Slug Marshall's grandson, but he wasn't sure. Between them was a scrawny girl with a large tattoo on one of her legs. She had one arm around Herm and the other arm was holding young Marshall in a headlock. They apparently didn't want anything to do with the bookstore, so they were heading toward the pier and beach area. Rex would later find out that young Marshall had decided against continuing his education so he was sharing some of his educational funds with crazy Herm and Herm's girlfriend.

The very last person to get off the bus was a girl dressed entirely in green who had obviously swallowed a watermelon seed and was about to give birth. Later, on the helicopter ride, Barry would tell Rex that Slim Simms was going to attempt the Iron Man and his wife, Shawna, in spite of the nearness of her time, wanted to be there for her husband.

The bookstore was hectic for the next few hours. It was very much a reunion for the ladies of the Dorcas Society who were all so proud of Eric Erickson for being a co-author of such a popular book. They were of course equally thrilled for Eleanor, whose son Barry was also going to compete in the Iron Man, since he considered this a good conditioning exercise.

After the Dorcas members had purchased their autographed books and enjoyed the punch that Tyler had provided, they returned to their bus for further touring of the island. While Eric was helping put away the displays and packing his belongings, Barry approached Rex who had attempted to maintain as low a profile as possible in the back of the small store.

Barry asked Rex if Tyler had some problems since there seemed to be something in his eyes which showed distress. Rex told Barry that Tyler's sister had a small business on Maui which was in the process of being lost to the evil Chinese landlord. Barry frowned and then mentioned that he would need to talk to Edna about that situation and also mentioned that he would be going to Maui along with the tour group for final conditioning exercises for the triathlon. Since Rex was also going to be a competitor, Barry thought it would be nice if Rex would go with them. Faith would also be going with her sponsors so Rex reluctantly agreed.

Barry then looked Rex straight in the eyes and said, "You know that Rex King is a redundancy, and people normally don't have names which are redundant. You probably would feel much better if you went by Rex Smalley." Rex felt himself blushing to the core, but in fact the blood was rushing away from his face and he was becoming very pale.

Barry then said, "Rosanne has been in jail for some time. After you disappeared, Dr. Kellem reappeared in town and immediately moved in with her. Apparently they had been seeing each other without your knowledge for some time. After you were gone a few weeks, Slug Marshall stopped by your house and when he went to help himself to some ice tea, he found human body parts cut and filleted throughout the freezer and refrigerator. Everyone assumed that Roseanne, and perhaps doc, took care of you and as a result, she has been spending her time in the basement of the courthouse. You probably should contact either judge Peck or M.L. Ullestad. Kellem again left town and Roseanne was arrested as she may or may not have known what he was doing. In any event, you will have to decide what is right and act accordingly."

Barry then reached down into one of the pockets of his fatigues and pulled out a video cassette. He placed it on the counter which separated the two men and then turned and walked out of the store with Eric.

Rex looked down and saw that the video was sitting on top of a copy of *Time* magazine. He put the cassette inside the magazine and took it across the street where he purchased a safe deposit box and locked up his million dollar prize.

53

THE SHAVED ICE SOLUTION

One of the local parishioners of the Evangelical Free Hawaiian Church loaned his oversized kayak to Faith. Thus, just after sunrise, the eight ladies of the Sam Hill Dorcas Society were assisted by Faith from the pier onto the long, thin boat. Additionally, Faith, Slug III, Herm and Summersalt Peters climbed aboard. Barry took a paddle and sat at the front and Rex had the other paddle at the back. Stroking in unison, the two men powerfully propelled the group away from the large island. The bright sun slowly rose behind them and the passengers enjoyed the light breeze created by the boat speeding over the water as the two muscular men powered them onward.

By mid-morning, the kayak was gliding into the sleepy village of Hana on the southeast corner of Maui. The itinerary that Faith had planned was that the group would browse through the quiet little village for a few hours and a mini van would then take them on the spectacular 50 mile drive around the corner of the island. The famous road to Hana, which in their case would be the road from Hana, has hairpin curves, less than single lanes of roadway at places and is definitely not recommended for driving after dark. Most people who drive to Hana find the experience so terrifying that they will heli-copter out of Hana and pay the rental company to fetch their automobiles and return them to the populated side of the island. Even Charles Lindberg, who navigated the Spirit of St. Louis all the way to Paris, found that his final trip to Hana was one way and his remains are now resting near the village.

Edna wanted to insure the safety of all of her friends and companions on the trip from Hana, so she arranged to have a special

207

driver available. This was why an old man with a patch over his glass eye was waiting on the dock to help lift the Dorcas Society members out of the kayak.

As most of the group grabbed their coin purses and headed for the trinket shops, Edna handed Barry a cardboard box and told him she would see him the next morning in Lahaina. At that time, he would lead them on a bicycle journey to the top of Mt. Haleakala, where they would spend a couple of hours with a picnic lunch and then bicycle back.

As Edna left to join the other ladies, Barry said to Rex, "You and I and Herm and his friends are scheduled to fly to the other side of the island. We will be leaving in a few minutes so you may want to keep an eye on them." Herm and Summersalt and Slug III were looking for a beach where they could wrestle, so Rex whistled and they quickly returned.

A few minutes later the small group was heading toward the helio pad. Barry was carrying the cardboard box. Rex was following close behind. Herm, in half a trance, was following Rex and Slug III and Summersalt were laughing and playing behind them. Slug would tickle Summersalt's ribs and she would reassert the headlock grip and scrub the top of Slug's head with her knuckles, causing him to squeal in delight.

They got on the Huey and Barry sat next to the pilot. Summersalt sat with her back to the pilot and facing Slug. Herm and Rex took the positions where the machine gunners would have been had they been still in Vietnam.

As the helicopter traversed the mountainous terrain and headed toward the western coast of the island, Herm seemed to sense an awareness of his surroundings that had been lacking for too long a time. Alternatively, he looked down at the ground and then back and forth at Barry and Rex. Then, smiling, he stood and unzipped his pants. He then turned and laughed loudly with Slug and Summersalt as his stream of urine was turned to mist by the strong winds.

After landing on the beach at Kehei, young Slug and

Summersalt and Herm frolicked in the water while Barry carried the box and together with Rex, marched across the street to Pilialoha's Shaved Ice and Ice Cream Shop. They jumped the two steps to the entrance and Barry sat the box in a corner. Rex took out his million dollar safe deposit box key. He knew that after selling the tape to Time magazine, he could easily bail out Pilialoha from her financial problems with the Chinese landlord, but something inside Rex kept urging him to mind his own business.

Barry introduced himself to Pilialoha and explained that her brother, Tyler, was a friend of his and that perhaps he could help her. At this exact moment, the Chinese landlord entered the premises with legal papers in hand and a menacing smile on his face. Pilialoha could not restrain her tears and soon she was sobbing so hard that she was gasping for air. Barry provided her with a handkerchief and then suggested to the landlord that an option may be available which, from a business perspective, would make more sense than closing the Shaved Ice and Ice Cream Shop.

Then Barry went to the box which was sitting in the corner and took out several t-shirts. The front and back of the t-shirts were as colorful as the rainbow. The t-shirts proclaimed in large letters that the Dorcas Society of Sam Hill and Pilialoha's Shaved Ice and Ice Cream Shop proudly sponsored athletes in the Iron Man Triathlon competition.

Barry gently reminded the Chinese businessman that hundreds of millions of viewers would see the event on ESPN and that all of the volunteers at the aid stations, the finish line officials and several of the top competitors would all be wearing either this t-shirt or one exactly like it which made no mention of Pilialoha's Shaved Ice and Ice Cream Shop. If the store were to be put out of business, the other shirts would be used and, of course, seen by the millions of viewers. On the other hand, if the astute businessman would agree to forego his rent money and allow Pilialoha to remain until business picked up, as it most certainly would after the Iron Man, then the brilliant Chinaman, who owned most of the ground within three blocks, would certainly become very wealthy because of the influx of tourism caused by the advertising on the t-shirts.

It took less than a minute for the Chinaman to see the wisdom of Barry's proposal. The landlord tore up the legal documents and Barry presented him with the first official t-shirt. Pilialoha then gave Barry and Rex a free lowfat dish of banana-pineapple-orange yogurt, which they ate while she answered the telephone.

Tyler had called her from the big island. Shawna Simms had gone into labor just as the kayak was leaving the big island and the ladies in the Dorcas Society would be pleased to know that she had just delivered a healthy baby boy. The only reason the child was not given a perfect ten on the AFGAR test was because he had a reddish colored birthmark on his right shoulder that was in the shape of a small hand. Barry assured Pilialoha that he would pass along this important information to Edna, who would insure that each member of the party was informed. Rex smiled, and rubbed his right shoulder with his left hand. At the same time he also shoved the million dollar safe deposit key deep into his pocket with his right hand.

Barry went next door to the bicycle rental shop where he rented a bike and took off to find the mini van, which at that very moment was negotiating a hairpin curve several hundred feet directly above the ocean. The passengers in the mini van were shrieking with delight as old glass-eyed Schumacher attempted to establish a new speed record to submit to the Guiness Book of World Records.

Rex walked on the beach, enjoying the sun and mentally starting to prepare himself for the Iron Man event. He became so absorbed in his thoughts that he did not hear Herm approach him from behind. He was therefore more than slightly startled when Herm called his name. "Rex, a blond lady who looks quite a bit like Faith just told me to give you a message. She said to meet her just after sunset on one of the white sand beaches near Kapalua. There will be a small bonfire so you will know where to go."

Herm was coherent when he spoke these words, and there was a glistening in his eyes which Rex had not seen since Herm's jeep left the base camp for the last time.

The two men stared at each other and Rex realized that the helicopter ride had somehow accomplished more than all the years of therapy. Rex could not hold back a trickle of tears that rolled down his face when Herm next spoke, indicating, among other things, the enormity of his progress in the few hours since the helicopter ride. "You know, Rex, everyone in the tour group thinks that you look much better now than when you were so big."

54

THE FINAL CHAPTER

The sun was dipping into the Pacific when Rex saw the bonfire. Leaving his sandals on, he walked down the beach to where the fire was crackling. A solitary young, thin, blond woman was feeding dried driftwood to the hungry fire. As the shadows disappeared and darkness overtook them, the woman motioned for Rex to sit on the edge of a blanket which was placed between the fire and the water's edge which slowly moved in with the coming tide.

Rex looked at her and said, "Is that you, Faith?"

She stopped feeding the fire and approached him. She replied, "No, and I don't have a twin sister either. My name is Verity and in a limited way, I am here to help you." She then returned to continue attending the fire.

Even though Rex was somewhat confused, he was beginning to think that this woman, or these women, were making him the recipient of some cruel, or at least awkward, joke. Sometime ago this prank may have been acceptable, but Rex had entirely too much in his favor now to put up with this behavior. After all, he had lost several hundred pounds, had a great head of hair, and had left his horrible wife and job far behind him. He even had a safe deposit key box that would assure him of enough money to last several lifetimes. He took the key out of his pocket and held it firmly in his strong right hand.

The woman was draped in a white dress. She glided around the fire and Rex noticed that she was so light that she left no footprints in the sand. In fact, only one set of footprints appeared. He still had his sandals, and was confused because there were no sandal prints.

Then, as the fire became so hot that Rex could feel the heat as it warmed his face several feet away, he felt the first tingle in his left arm. It felt as if he had been sleeping on it all night and he shook it to get rid of the pin pricks. As he did this, he noticed his left leg and part of his face also start to tingle. He tried to stand, but realized that paralysis was nearly complete on the left side of his body.

Verity turned to him and said, "Don't worry, it will not hurt. You might be more comfortable if you lie down."

Obediently, Rex positioned himself on the ground with his numbed left side against the ground. He faced the fire and listened to the ocean lapping to the shore behind him. He gazed at the sand a few inches from his face and then looked at the sky which was now filling with stars.

It was incredibly unbelievable. There was no way he could be having a stroke, or a heart attack or whatever it was that was happening to him. He was too young for this. He was just getting his life back in order. This could not possibly be happening. He clutched the safe deposit box key so hard that it cut the palm of his hand. There must be more time left because he hadn't negotiated the deal yet with the magazine for the assassination film. But the numbness would not go away and he could not move.

Rex called out to the woman, "Verity, tell me, how can this be happening? Please make this go away. You can have my safe deposit key. Anything. Please help me."

She came close to where he was lying. She squatted down on her haunches and softly whispered to him, "What is the most important thing that has ever happened to you?"

Rex was breathing heavily. If he had any chance at all to live, he must have her help so he thought about how he should respond to her. He felt his body relaxing and his mind became more at ease as he thought of her question. Finally, he said, "There was a revival at Sam Hill. I sat on a hill with many other people and listened to Ben Sardinhurst proclaim the gospel. I had a spiritual experience and was baptized. I felt renewed more on that day than any other day in my life."

The woman again whispered to him, "What happened?"

Rex thought about it for a few moments and then replied, "Things got worse instead of better. Even though that was a great day, it was like the bonfire in front of me. I felt it was roaring but it soon burned itself out.

"Since my accident and since I have been living in the mission with Faith and the other missionaries and students, I have been much closer to that day back in Sam Hill. I really feel that I am doing something with my life and I want to do the Iron Man next weekend because I know it will be the greatest achievement of my life."

Verity moved closer to Rex's right ear and again whispered even more softly, "Rex, no matter what you have done or failed to do; no matter what you think is of great importance; nothing, absolutely nothing that has happened before is of any consequence compared to what is about to happen."

Rex could not lift his head but his eyes followed her as she stood up, turned and stood next to the fire. She then softly blew him a kiss and put her outstretched arms over the flames. Rex saw the fire pull her inward and upward and she disappeared and evaporated into the smoke which rose above the flames.

Rex lay silently, being aware only of the gentle wind, water lapping closer and closer to him, fire blazing before him and the sand and earth below him. Finally, he looked upward and saw the glowing stars becoming brighter and brighter.

Rex accepted the fact that he no longer had control over anything. He felt drool ooze out of his mouth and drip onto the blanket below. The paralysis had now spread everywhere except his right arm. The only thing he could feel was the key which he squeezed over and over and over.

There was so much that was yet unfinished.

Rosanne in jail.

So what?

He could have helped Pilialoha.

He was still relieved that the Saint had died.

He wondered how well Herm would get.

Why was he able to have visions when other people couldn't?

How long would the bonfire burn?

When the tide comes in completely, would it drown him?

Would his new watch continue to run if he were washed
out to sea?

Rex could still hear out of his right ear and although his left eye was now fixed and dilated, his right eye still could see. He pulled his right arm close to his face. The key dropped from his hand. He looked at his new watch and saw that at that exact moment the second hand froze and the watch stopped working.

At first he thought his hearing was completely gone. Then he realized that the water was no longer splashing against the shore. The fire no longer crackled and in fact, the flame was frozen in mid air. There was no movement of any kind. Rex did not fully comprehend what was happening, but time had stopped throughout the entire universe.

Next to Rex's mouth an invisible megaphone extended funnel like outward into the cosmos.

It was the moment of truth for Rex. Eternity depended on what would happen next. The decision that he had to make, his final and only important decision, was so vital that all of creation, throughout all dimensions of time, space, energy and existence, stopped.

Rex dropped his right arm to the blanket and tried to hoist himself up. The remaining last bit of energy was sapped and the arm fell limp, becoming numb like the rest of his body. There no longer was a need for his remaining senses and he felt his hearing and remaining eyesight gradually fade. There was no longer any reason to breath so his chest subsided in its movement.

Then, after what could have been either a millisecond or a hundred million years, three words barely gurgled from Rex's throat.

The first word, which could not have been heard by any living being more than a few inches away from his mouth, tumbled through the megaphone, gaining speed and force as it shot through the galaxies and universes and into the farthest reaches of space. As the word unleased its immeasurable force, its power smashed into a star many times larger than our sun and the collision destroyed the star causing it to burst into billions and billions of fireballs which floated throughout expanses of space which were an indeterminable number of light years from the origin.

COME

The second word was even more faint as it came from Rex's throat. It barely crawled into the invisible megaphone but like the first word, it gained momentum and force as it hurled its way through eons of time and space. It rolled so fast that it echoed off recorded history and bounced forward into a time zone where the last man would breath his last breath. Cymbals crashed, drums rolled and the voices of all ages joined in the Hallelujah Chorus.

LORD

The sweet release of mortality accompanied the final word from his throat and out his rigid mouth. As that last word escaped him, a grain of sand was picked up by the breeze and was dropped into the fire which started again burning. The waves moved closer to the carcass that was now left on the beach and the living creatures upon the earth were once again in motion, not realizing that a special event had taken place for one of their fellow creatures and that some day such a special event would be theirs.

As the earth again started to rotate, the final word was speeding outward pulling along a soul to a new beginning, where tears and worries and sadness did not exist.

JESUS

55

CARL'S COMA

.....The emptiness that was inside Carl after Angel was buried was intolerable. His reason for living, the essence of his being and his entire existence ceased to be. There was a small degree of comfort in the oral satisfaction of feeling a pipe stem, cigar or cigarette entrenched in the vacant spot in his mouth. Watching the smoke expel from his body, Carl could visualize the haze and cloudiness which was now his life. He neglected his health and merely went through the motions at work until even his work which he had always enjoyed, became work, then he put in for early retirement. His waking hours were then spent sitting sullenly at the same kitchen table which for so many joyous mealtimes had provided support for the weight of his and his beloved Angel's bodies.

Finally, on a Sunday night, he fell into the coma and nearly died. Ever since the trial of Dr. Kellem, Carl and Angel had good naturedly joked about the collagen which was placed in the soup at Campbell's diner. Soupy had been a true entrepreneur with one of the few thriving businesses in Sam Hill because not only did his famous soup taste superior to that purchased at the market, but it gave a youthful appearance to those who drank it and to those who preferred to use the liquid as a face cream. However, as soon as the ingredients to the tasty soup was disclosed, Soupy left town and his famous soup was never again eaten. Angel had put away the Carlson's private stock of the soup and on occasions when Carl felt very melancholy, he would take a can of the soup and eat it while remembering the days of his union with Angel. On the day of the coma he had barely started the soup when he lost consciousness and the right side of his face dropped into the soup where it was submerged for several hours until Penelope Peaks happened by and got help. From that time on for the rest of Carl's life, the premature wrinkles and shadows under his right eye were cleared even though the left side of his face continued to show the aging process.

No one knew how long Carl would remain in the coma, so Edna told Dr. Goodman that she felt it was her duty to provide a room for him at her retirement home. After all, although Carl had never told her, she knew that at the time of Alexander's death, that Carl had vainly tried to jump in front of Alexander and take the bullet himself. She also knew that Carl's valiant attempt to save Alexander had failed, but he must have been in the fox hole with Alexander and cradled him in his arms and helped him through the fear of losing his life.

Carl was given a spacious room with a window that faced Edna's pond. A surveillance camera was placed in his room with continuous tapings so that if he did stir from the coma the nursing station would be aware. The ladies of the Dorcas Society stopped by frequently and included Carl in their weekly prayers at the basement of the Methodist church. Eleanor Sardinhurst, whose hair was now turning the same color as her friends, made a permanent note on her prayer sheet to insure that Carl would be included each week until such time as he recovered.

Carl did not recover as hoped. As the days dragged into weeks, it seemed that the prayers were not being answered and the nursing skills of Rachel Sardinhurst and Carolyn Johnson-Rogers-Goodman were not working. Eventually, an oxygen tent was draped over Carl's bed and no smoking signs were placed on each wall of the room.

Although Carl could never be accused of being a dreamer or visionary, his mind at times was active while his body was not. Because Carl had become a chain smoker many of the things which went about in his head related to heat, smoke and fire. A few did not.

One of the first dreams that Carl had while in the coma was about the fire at the corncob pile on the outskirts of town. Carl's shiny orange and white volunteer firemans helmet floated before him as he followed Slug Marshall to the scene. Vaguely, and through a dense smoky haze, he saw Slug lift his son off Barry Sardinhurst's back and watched the smiling youthful Sardinhurst fade from the dream. His attention was transferred to the cob pile and again he watched the huge mountain of cobs crackle and explode with the tremendous heat generated by the flames. The dream seemed to continue as long as the original fire. Carl could see the skies turn from sunshine to darkness, enhancing the wonder of the bright red flames. He could see the cheerleaders kicking and high stepping in front of the homecoming rally which was held close to the blaze. All of his friends and fellow townsman, appearing much younger, were assembled with folding chairs in the evening so that they could gaze at the spectacular fire.

The huge mountain of cobs and the volcanic affect of the hot flames receded and Dr. Kellem walked toward Carl. He was staring at Carl and drinking tomato soup from a porcelain bowl. The soup was dripping down his face and out of his spittle laden mouth came reassuring words to Carl that the soup was very tasty and Carl should drink some through a straw which would fit perfectly in the empty space of his mouth. Kellem then handed Carl an advertisement from the Sam Hill Clarion. The ad declared that Carl and other smokers in Sam Hill would soon be cured of their nicotine habit. Carl, with his orange and white volunteer fireman's helmet floating before him, saw that his hands and legs were shackled and that he was being pulled by High Pockets to a hotel in Des Moines where the horse galloped to the third floor, dragging Carl behind.

Tom Kellem, a college graduate trying to earn money for medical school, opened the door and with a crooked finger, beckoned Carl inside. Kellem guaranteed Carl that for the paltry sum of three hundred dollars, the nicotine desires would be forever banished. Kellem then pulled the money from Carl's helmet and extended a soupy hand to Carl to seal the agreement.

Kellem explained the instructions in detail and admonished Carl that the cure would only work if Carl followed the directions without deviation. He had to come to the hotel room every morning for one week. He would be there for one hour and during that period of time he could smoke his favorite brand of cigarette. However, he could not smoke at any other time during the day. Within a week he would be cured.

The following day Carl showed up at the hotel with two packs of cigarettes. Kellem told him to sit on the bed in the middle of the room. The bed had no coverings over the mattress, but there were two ashtrays. Kellem then took a plastic cover which went over the bed and down to the other side so that Carl was confined to a tent like atmosphere. Kellem lifted up the clear plastic covering and attached small wires to Carl's wrists. He then told Carl to start chain smoking. Each time that Carl would light a match, Kellem would send staccato like electrical shock waves into Carl's body. Whenever a cigarette touched his mouth, the same thing happened. Whenever he tried to draw the wonderful smoke into his lungs, he would get a double shot to remind him not to inhale the smoke. If he did not puff fast enough, Kellem would yell at him to speed up so that he could give him more shocks of electricity. After five or six cigarettes in twenty-five minutes, Carl wanted to escape from the madness. However, Kellem reminded him of the agreement and that there would be no refund. The smoke was so thick and stale within the confined area that Carl nearly vomited. After the first hour, he thought he would never want to see a cigarette again.

That week Carl thought that a concentration camp would have been preferable to Kellem's torture chamber. However, the treatment was successful and Carl's mind finally evacuated the smoke-filled hotel.

In his continuing dream life, Carl lived constantly on chewing gum and candy bars and abstinence from coffee in an effort not to renew his desires for the smokes. He would see billboards as he followed his helmet down the road in his buggy and the billboards would extol the virtues of smoking. He would stop in front of Sal's barbershop and would watch the television through the pane glass window. He had seen very little television in his life and in fact had never seen it during the time that he was with Angel. Now, he stared at it for weeks at a time through Sal's window. Every television show seemed to be sponsored by the old gold tap dancing girl where her long thin legs extended from the cigarette box. Whenever he looked around, Carl saw people smoking and enjoying it and seemingly blowing smoke toward his face to spite him.

Suddenly he was at Wrigley Field and the ushers brought a large birthday cake. It was in the shape of a baseball diamond with a bat and ball covering the outfield. Candles were on the edge of the cake signifying the new lighting system which was to be put in the ballpark. As the ushers lighted the candles, Carl gazed at the flagpole in left field. A large parachute with the number fourteen was waving from the top of the pole. Attached to the pole was an old gray mare which was suffocating from the smoke which was being blown at her from the candles.

Carl had two choices, he could either let the old horse choke to death from the smoke or he could sacrifice himself and pick up the candles, which had now turned to cigarettes, and smoke them himself, encasing the fumes inside his lungs and saving the horse. As he contemplated his next move, he coughed.

Carl coughed so hard that it woke him from the coma. His first sensation was that his throat was parched. Something was stuck in his nostrils blowing cold air through his nose. He started to reach toward his face but his hand, like the rest of his body, had been asleep so long that he could not yet move. He thought he was inside his tent on Diamond Head, but looking through his nearly transparent tent, he saw walls. He distinguished signs on one wall. He tried to focus his eyes, and was dismayed when he saw the words

NO SMOKING

Carl still had not moved. The oxygen that had been pouring into him made his head clearer, but the rest of his body was tormented. He tried to speak, but the dried spittle had glued his mouth shut. It tasted like the Russian army had marched barefoot through his mouth. He wondered why he had come out of the coma and he wished that he could go back into it. But more than that he craved a cigarette. Then, a few minutes later, his cravings gave way to his wishes and he re-entered the coma.

Carl had no more dreams, but when he finally was aroused from the coma, the cravings were gone as was the depression and unhealthy feeling that he had maintained since Angel's death. For when he woke up, there, helping him find peace, curled up on his stomach, was Penelope Peaks.

56

THE TALE OF THE TAPE

The word had barely gotten around town that Carl had come out of his coma when Monica Monroe stopped by M.L. Ullestad's office at the courthouse. Ullestad initially had no idea what type of city or county business that the pleasant looking nurse from Edna's could be about, so he invited her in for a private consultation and closed the door to his office. Unfortunately for M.L., who is not used to spending conference time with such visually pleasurable young women, Monica was not prepared for small talk.

She immediately told M.L. that she was new to the nursing field and had observed something on the surveillance camera in Carl's room that was very disturbing. She did not want to start any scandals and was afraid to discuss this with her co-employees, Carolyn Johnson-Rogers-Goodman and Rachel Sardinhurst. Also, she did not want to take this to her boss, Edna. In fact she was very uncomfortable with what had transpired on the camera and did not even want to discuss it with M.L. She then pulled out a video tape, placed it on his desk and gently moved it toward him. If, after viewing it, he thought that any laws had been broken or prosecution should be pursued, then, and only then, would she be willing to become involved. With that, she abruptly ended the conference, stood and did an about face, and escorted herself out of the county attorney's office.

The first thing M.L. did was wad up a piece of paper and toss it through the window which was over the door and onto his secretary's desk. He then informed her that the previous appointment was for official business and that it should be logged accordingly.

He had not used the video machine in his office since he received the bizarre tape from Barry Sardinhurst. Ullestad had heard enough about the Kennedy assassination over the years and had seen enough photographs of it to last him a lifetime. He still couldn't figure out why Sardinhurst had given him a copy of the movie and M.L. absentmindedly wondered if he had kept or thrown away that strange tape.

At any rate, Ullestad thought that this new case may prove to be interesting, especially if it would result in further interviews with Ms. Monroe.

That afternoon Ullestad ran and re-ran the tape many times. It was very clear that it was Penelope Peaks who had entered Carl's room. She was wearing what appeared to be a terry cloth robe and she stood by his bed for several minutes. Ullestad could then clearly see that she took a deep breath and then lifted the covering which enveloped his bed. As the clarity of her form became distorted by the oxygen tent covering, something fell to the floor but try as he might, Ullestad could not determine if it was Penelope's robe or one of the sheets from the bottom of the bed. Penelope's form disappeared completely as her body went under the covers. For the next several minutes it was impossible to tell what, if anything, was transpiring under those covers but eventually Ullestad could ascertain the movement of Carl's hands as they reached toward the ceiling in the same way that Ullestad had seen Pentecostals raise their hands in church service. It was at this point that the video tape ran out.

Monica, who was in charge of monitoring the cameras, was tending to Mr. Schumacher and did not put in a new tape until after the room was vacated by Penelope.

A few days later Ullestad decided to pay Monica a visit. Upon arriving at the retirement home he was disappointed to find that she had the day off. Rachel was busy settling arguments over who would get to ride with Mr. Schumacher at the next pond races, so Carolyn Johnson-Rogers-Goodman poured M.L.'s coffee, which he sipped on while waiting for Edna to return from the meeting of the

Dorcas Society.

Eventually, M.L. and Edna were sitting in Edna's homey office. M.L. could see that Monica had learned the traits of her boss when Edna rushed through the small talk and approached what she thought was the reason for Ullestad's visit.

"M.L., I assume you are here to talk about the problem with Carl."

M.L., seizing upon the opportunity to gain information which was not clearly shown on the tape, and not wanting to show his ignorance of what transpired, gave a knowing nod and looked at Edna, urging her to continue.

"Well, M.L., Slug Marshall stopped by a couple days ago and as I told him, taking one little barricade that belongs to the city does not seem like that much of a big deal." Edna looked at M.L., seeking confirmation, but only a blank stare was returned.

Obviously M.L. was not convinced that such a small matter should be dismissed as a prank, so she continued, "When Carl came out of his coma, he wanted Penelope to move into his room with him. Since they are not married, such a situation would contradict the rules of this establishment. Personally, having been around a long time, and being widowed like Penelope and even Carl, I could understand a slight deviation from the rules, at least until they could go through the formal ceremony of a marriage, if that's what they both wanted.

"The nurses, being a generation younger in the case of Rachel and Carolyn, were very upset by Carl's request to have Penelope with him. Even Monica, poor young thing that she is, didn't know what to make of the situation and in fact refused to let Penelope stay with Carl. Penelope then came to the nurses station and showed all of us the wedding band which was placed on her finger by Carl. It was really an aluminum pop top ring which as far as they were concerned was as legitimate as a diamond.

"Here poor Carl, barely out of the coma, was, according to the staff's way of thinking, being seduced by his own neighbor lady who knew absolutely nothing about him or what would be good for him. The more that the staff and myself encouraged Penelope to wait, the more hostile the situation was for us, especially since the residents were unanimous in support of Carl and Penelope.

"Then, after we managed to keep Penelope out of Carl's room the first night after his coma was over, Carl slipped away for a few hours and apparently went to the maintenance shop at city garage. He still had keys to the garage and he apparently brought back the barricade which he would use at night to wedge against his door to lock himself and Penelope in. And then, during the day he would loan it to whichever of the residents needed a walker for the day and the residents have been taking turns using this stylish new walker with a flashing yellow light.

"Slug told me that not only has Carl been guilty of breaking and entering, but there could be a theft charge and several violations of the safety code for nursing homes when Carl locks himself in at night with Penelope. I really thought Slug was overreacting and if you are here to pursue criminal charges, I would suggest again that they are too petty to fool with and secondly that every resident in this nursing home would be picketing the courthouse over the injustice of any charges that might be filed."

M.L. put his empty cup on the small table that separated the two, and stood and moved toward the doorway. Before leaving, he turned toward Edna and questioned, "Just how are they doing anyway?"

Without hesitation, Edna said, "As long as we leave them alone, Penelope and Carl are happier than red-winged blackbirds at the end of mating season."

M.L. looked at the hardwood floor and half muttered, "I get your drift, Edna."

57

A SHORT SAD CHAPTER

It was the best of times at Edna's retirement home. Edna instructed her staff to honor the vows of monogamy taken by Carl and Penelope, as demonstrated by the aluminum ring which remained upon Penelope's finger. Over the next few weeks more barricades mysteriously appeared at the nursing home. At first Edna thought that some of her more elderly residents were requiring assistance in ambulating, but it soon became obvious to her that the barricades were also used to insure nocturnal privacy for the married residents who had been given separate rooms for various reasons which now were not considered valid by those involved. In fact, Edna noticed that the home took on a new buoyant atmosphere that it had never previously had.

In the center of all these changes was the always present face of Carl Carlson, with an always smiling face displaying a gaping hole in his mouth where two teeth had long since been gone, and an old withered left profile and a smooth wrinkle-free youthful right side.

Then, as suddenly as Carl's new life had begun, like a lake that cleanses and purifies itself once a year by turning its water over, it ended. Penelope arrived early one morning at the nurses station with tear stained cheeks that would have reminded Carl of the way Angel had looked when she told him of her illness. Softly, nearly inaudibly, in a whispering monotone, Penelope told Monica, "A few minutes ago Carl told me how lucky he was to have had two loves in his life; then he squeezed my hand, and died."

58

MORNING MOURNING
REVISITED

Ben turned to the group of mourners. He knew that some of the mourners had come to hear the words of salvation and comfort. Others had come to pay their last respects to Carl and some of the younger people were there for the food, fishing and other festivities which would transpire later in the day. The music had been inspirational and Ben felt the calling to preach with a conviction that he had not felt since the day of the conversions following the revival near the bridge.

Ben thought about his speaking through the megaphone while Barry bungy jumped into the burning bridge to save Slug III and how the wind had positioned it perfectly and the rain had come and put out the fire and all of the other things that had happened that day. Ben even remembered seeing huge Rex Smalley on the hillside raising his hand in acceptance when the alter call to the river was announced. He did not remember seeing Carl that day, but try as he might, Ben could not ever remember seeing Carl other than coaching on Saturday mornings and running back and forth to work each day from the house on Baker Street across from which Ben had lived all of his life. A slight smile broke across Ben's face as he remembered his other recollection of Carl, which was when Carl was fluttering in the breeze high above Wrigley Field. The more Ben thought, the more he knew it would be difficult to spend much time on the eulogy since Carl's life had indeed been rather mundane.

A spirit welled up inside Ben as he began his sermon. He told the crowd of the wondrous plan of eternal life that was in store for all believers. He assured them that their childlike faith in the atonement of sin by Christ would insure eternal rewards far more magnificent than any earthly pleasure which they may have known. The twenty-third Psalm is considered mandatory at Jewish funerals, but discretionary at Christian burials. Ben thought that the words of the Psalmist were appropriate in Carl's case and he led the mourners through the Valley of the Shadow of Death, thus leading into the eulogy and Carl's close calls in the far away Pacific and the much nearer areas of Chicago and his own swing set. As Ben mentioned Carl's soldiering in the second great war, Edna dabbed tears from her eyes as she recalled how heroically Carl had nearly saved Grover and had actually been able to carry him back to the safety of the beach where a Chaplain no doubt was able to administer soothing words of comfort to Grover and assure Grover of his home with the Lord before he died.

Ben told the crowd how Carl had lived the Christian life to the very end and how he was predeceased by his wife, Angel, to whom he had been faithful throughout his life. Penelope could feel her jaws tighten and her teeth grind as she heard these words, but she knew that the youthful preacher quite probably did not know and could not understand the twists and turns in Carl's experiencing the fullness of life. She also knew, based on her life long friendship with Angel, that in a way Ben's words were mostly true.

Ben toiled too long on Carl's coaching endeavors. However, this was understandable since this was the only personal relationship that existed between the decedent and the minister. A few words were mentioned about the flagpole and guide wire at Wrigley Field, and this antidote brought smiles and chuckles to the otherwise solemn crowd. Ben then concluded the funeral with what was later discussed in Sal's barbershop as a brilliant finish. He reminded the crowd of Carl's influence on the youngsters to the little league program and observed that Rex Smalley had probably left Sam Hill to go to Hawaii because of the stories which Carl had told to the boys. The story of Rex's death had been chronicled in a book by two local authors, Eric Erickson and Phyllis Noble.

The crowd then sat spellbound as Ben read to them the following edited passages concerning the transition of life into eternity:

"Time had stopped throughout the entire universe. Next to his mouth an invisible megaphone extended funnel like outward into the cosmos.

It was the moment of truth. Eternity depended on what would happen next. The decision that he had to make, his final and only important decision, was so vital that all of creation, throughout all dimensions of time, space, energy and existence, stopped. Then, after what could have been either a millisecond or a hundred million years, three words barely gurgled from his throat.

The first word, which could not have been heard by any living being more than a few inches away from his mouth, tumbled through the megaphone, gaining speed and force as it shot through the galaxies and universes and into the farthest reaches of space. As the word unleased its immeasurable force, its power smashed into a star many times larger than our sun and the collision destroyed the star causing it to burst into billions and billions of fireballs which floated throughout expanses of space which were an indeterminable number of light years from the origin.

COME

The second word was even more faint as it came from his throat. It barely crawled into the invisible megaphone but like the first word, it gained momentum and force as it hurled its way through eons of time and space. It rolled so fast that it echoed off recorded history and bounced forward into a time zone where the last man would breath his last breath. Cymbals crashed, drums rolled and the voices of all ages joined in the Hallelujah Chorus.

LORD

The sweet release of mortality accompanied the final word from his throat and out his rigid mouth. As that last word escaped him, the living creatures upon the earth were once again in motion, not realizing that a special event had taken place for one of their fellow creatures and that some day such a special event would be theirs. As the earth again started to rotate, the final word was speeding outward pulling along a soul to a new beginning, where tears and worries and sadness did not exist.

JESUS"

Ben closed the book. He then put a marker in his Bible and closed it also. In parting, he told the crowd to go forward with their lives but not to forget those who had gone before them.

No one moved as Ben turned and led all eyes toward the large cross on the Catholic side of the cemetery. Once again, the cross started changing hues from white to red to yellow to red again and then back to white. Again Ben felt the electrical charge exuding from the crowd which watched in amazement. The funeral, though impressive, had not changed the hearts of those in attendance. The strong believers still knew that the old cross changing colors was a sign from God. The less strong were only thankful to be witnesses to what appeared to be a miraculous event. The only difference was that the smug skeptics, who knew that Slug III was again playing with the flashers in the police car which was parked out of their view, were wrong. In fact, the young man was worn out by the lengthy sermon and was curled up on the ground near Edna's fishing pond with his head on Summersalt Peter's lap, fast asleep.